I0833673

Rise Up

A Call to Action for Men of God

Connor Boyack

SOCIAL HARMONY

To Joseph Smith

For setting the example and charting the course.

Social Harmony
2183 W. Main #A102
Lehi, UT 84043

Rise Up: A Call to Action for Men of God

ISBN-13 979-8-88688-049-6 (paperback)

CONTENTS

Other religious titles by the author:

The Slow Stain: Lessons from the Past, Warnings for Today

Christ versus Caesar: Two Masters, One Choice

Latter-day Responsibility: Choosing Liberty through Personal Accountability

Latter-day Liberty: A Gospel Approach to Government and Politics

PREFACE

"The world is calling for women of vision and courage," wrote Harriot Stanton Blatch in her 1940 memoirs. "May the women of the world hear the call and go forward!"[1] Like her mother, Harriott had risen to prominence as an outspoken advocate of women's rights and was particularly prominent during the suffrage movement a few decades earlier. In 1907, she founded the Equality League for Self-Supporting Women, comprised of some 20,000 women who were employed as factory, garment, and laundry workers. But her big break came on May 21, 1910.

Some 10,000 New Yorkers gathered in Union Square to demand that women receive the ability to vote. Harriot had every right to be pleased with herself—this was the largest suffrage demonstration yet held in the country, building on years of work by female activists who had been privately plotting, strategizing, lobbying, and increasingly speaking out publicly. Each woman standing up for herself seemed to give another courage to do the same. As more went public with their demands, they formed a web of organizations to advance their cause—groups such as the National

---

1 Harriot Stanton Blatch, *Challenging Years: The Memoirs of Harriot Stanton Blatch* (Pennsylvania State University, 1940), 335.

American Woman Suffrage Association, the Women's Political Union, the Equal Franchise Society, the National Woman's Party, and more. The broader effort to further women's causes led to a proliferation of nonpolitical organizations as well; this period of women empowerment produced ladies' aid societies, women's missionary societies, Bible study groups for women, mothers' meetings, female-only fraternal organizations, literary clubs, social clubs, and others.

Men had their own organizations, of course, and as with the women, many of them were religious in nature. Different Christian denominations had their own groups, such as the Brotherhood of Saint Andrew for the Episcopal Church; the Knights of Columbus for Catholic men; the Lutheran Brotherhood; the Methodist Brotherhood; the Men's Fellowship of the Baptist Church; and the Presbyterian Brotherhood. Many of them were quite recently formed. For example, the Presbyterian Brotherhood held its first convention in November 1906. A committee of pastors at the convention described what had led them to organize together:

> The present movement for the organization of men's societies for Christian work... was made the subject of a notable paper read at the Congress of Religions that was held [during] the World's Fair in Chicago in 1893. This gave great impetus to the movement in nearly all evangelical denominations. Many of our pastors welcomed this impetus, organized men's clubs or leagues, most of which aimed specially at increasing the effectiveness of the Sunday evening services.

> The existence of these organizations was brought to the attention of the Assembly... in 1895 in the following terms: "The call is made for the organization of men. The men of our church, as a class, are falling to the rear of the great host of God in both service and benevolence. This occurs largely because they are not organized into associations as the women are. To evangelize men, to pray and labor for their salvation, is the need of the hour, second to no other call in the sphere of Christian work."[2]

William Merrill was a Presbyterian pastor in Chicago at the time but did not attend the convention. And there's no indication that he was preoccupied with these gender-specific causes nor involved with the Brotherhood—but his friend Nolan was. Nolan Best was editor of *The Continent*, a Presbyterian newspaper in Chicago, and was a faithful attendee at the Brotherhood's conventions. At the fourth one, held in February 1911, he gave a rousing speech to his fellow attendees, calling for more engaged and faithful men to act as Christians:

> How we have felt the importance of teaching the men in our community the Bible—practically as it relates to twentieth century life! How we have felt the stress of promoting this Men and Religion Forward Movement in our towns! How we have felt the absolute, the essential, importance of a personal evangelism, man to man! How we have felt the importance of this as it touches the saving of the whole man! How we have

2 *Presbyterian Brotherhood: Report of the First Convention* (Philadelphia: The Presbyterian Board of Publication, 1907), 7.

> been stirred with the determination to do something for the boys of the community! Now let us do it.[3]

Best decided that what the Brotherhood really needed in order to unify in their common cause was a song—a hymn to serve as a sort of rallying cry. He mentioned this desire to Merrill, who later wrote that "the suggestion lingered in my mind"[4] until he soon came upon an article titled "The Church of the Strong Men," in which the author called for mighty men to build churches in the great cities to foster stronger communities and a unified, strong Christian world. "The reason that so many of our most typical and successful and commanding men today are not going to church," the article's author wrote, "is that a bodiless church does not interest them."[5] It wasn't enough to learn doctrine and recite scripture—the point of church, the author argued, was to embody the spirit and strength necessary to command respect and influence in society. Christianity needed strong men to move its cause forward—a "bodied" church that could engage with the concerns of people's daily lives.

Stirred by the article's powerful call to action, Merrill's thoughts spontaneously transformed into the lyrics of a hymn that perfectly captured the spirit of strength and unity that Best and the Brotherhood longed to champion. Merrill would

---

3 *Presbyterian Men: Addresses and Proceedings of the Fourth National Convention* (Chicago: The Presbyterian Brotherhood of America, 1911), 377.

4 Calvin Weiss Laufer, *Hymn Lore* (Philadelphia: The Westminster Press, 1932), 132.

5 Gerald Stanley Lee, "The Church of the Strong Men," *The Outlook*, February 4, 1905.

later write that "suddenly this hymn came up, almost without conscious thought or effort."[6] It was created first as a poem titled "To the Brotherhood," published in Best's *The Continent,* and published as a hymn in 1912. From there, it spread quickly and was adopted by Christian men in a variety of denominations. The lyrics read:

> 1. *Rise up, O men of God!*
> *Have done with lesser things.*
> *Give heart and mind and soul and strength*
> *to serve the King of kings.*
>
> 2. *Rise up, O men of God!*
> *His kingdom tarries long.*
> *Bring in the day of brotherhood*
> *and end the night of wrong.*
>
> 3. *Rise up, O men of God!*
> *The church for you doth wait,*
> *her strength unequal to her task;*
> *rise up, and make her great!*
>
> 4. *Lift high the cross of Christ!*
> *Tread where his feet have trod.*
> *As brothers of the Son of Man,*
> *rise up, O men of God!*

As a member of The Church of Jesus Christ of Latter-day Saints, I've heard this hymn since I was a child, and as a young man, I sang it proudly and loudly with fellow missionaries—

---

6 Laugher, *Hymn Lore*, 132.

men of God rising up to do as Christ commanded. Yet it wasn't until much later in life that I discovered that the Church's hymnal omits the third verse. For reasons I'll explore later in this book, it's entirely absent. The second line of the second verse was also changed, from "His kingdom tarries long" to "in one united throng." Thus, we sing a condensed and revised version of Merrill's poem. Ours is not the only denomination to alter Merrill's text; however, while in some cases the hymnals of other churches also omit the third verse, many also generalize the call to action beyond only men. "Rise up, Ye Saints of God" is how one popular usage reads. Another replaces it with "church of God," referring to all Christians collectively. This alteration is borne out of a seemingly widespread sentiment that Merrill's original lyrics were sexist. One author cataloguing the "feminization" of American hymns observed:

> "Rise Up, O Men of God" draws some of its figurative language from a sexuality intent upon domination and display of power. The hymn presents "men of God" as having a machismo that glories in an erection of strength and the impregnation (making great with child) of a feeble woman, which is the way Merrill describes the church in stanza three.[7]

The author further argues that Merrill's original hints at a "submission to sexual authority" in furtherance of "a renewed and vigorous masculinity."[8] But none of this was what Merrill

---

7 June Hadden Hobbs, *"I Sing for I Cannot Be Silent": The Feminization of American Hymnody*, 1870-1920 (Pittsburgh: The University of Pittsburgh Press, 1997), 98-99.

8 Ibid.

was suggesting: his was not a call to subjugate women in order to elevate men who glory in "an erection of strength." Surely he would have found such an analysis to be preposterous. He wasn't trying to discriminate against women, but to challenge men.

Reviewing Merrill's teachings, one cannot find any implied sexism beyond simply adopting the masculine term to refer to everyone; saying "men" is often mere shorthand for referring to all. When Merrill later wrote that the church's chief end is "perpetually calling men to be souls and not cogs,"[9] or when he referred to the "grace of God which he offers to all men,"[10] or when he mentioned that Christ's salvation comes "to all men who hear him,"[11] he was clearly not excluding women—just as scripture itself often uses the masculine as a catch-all to imply everyone. Historically, the masculine form has been used as the default or "unmarked" gender in most Indo-European languages. This means that the masculine form is often used when the gender is unknown, mixed, or irrelevant. For instance, in English, words like "mankind" or "man" have traditionally been used to refer to all of humanity, not just males.

But like some of his critics have done, let's take Merrill's lyrics at face value and assume, for purposes of this book, that his was a call specifically and directly to men. This is not unreasonable since the focused intent of his authorship was to support the Brotherhood's rallying of men—despite the prin-

---

9 William Pierson Merrill, *The Freedom of the Preacher* (New York: The Macmillan Company, 1922), 10.

10 Ibid., 138.

11 Ibid., 136.

ciples and doctrines applying, of course, to women as well. Merrill's use of the masculine form was not a statement of superiority—it was a strategic choice to engage a demographic that, as noted earlier, had been identified as lagging in participation and commitment within the church. It was, put simply, a call for men to "man up" and do their duty.

What, then, are the "lesser things" that trouble men today and impede their discipleship? What does it look like for a father and husband to give his "heart and mind and soul and strength" to serve God in a busy world already imposing heavy responsibilities on his shoulders? What lurks in the shadows of the "night of wrong," and how can a Christian brotherhood of men resist and repel it? What role do men play today in building up the influence and power of the Church, if indeed "her strength [is] unequal to her task." And what exactly does it look like for men today to tread where Jesus' feet have trod? Flowery, poetic language has its place to evoke emotion and imagination. The task of this book is to bring such airy prose to a firmer foundation, with practical examples of how men today ought to act in order to rise up in a world full of people who are content with lying low.

My first book, *Latter-day Liberty*, was a tremendous success. Published in 2011, that book's message struck a chord with my audience—helping readers learn about what the gospel of Jesus Christ says about government and politics. Its thesis was relevant and provocative (and timely, given the attention Mitt Romney's failed presidential campaign brought to the intersection of Mormonism and politics). A few months after publication, while in the car running errands,

I had downloaded into my mind—"almost without conscious thought or effort," to echo Merrill's words—the entire structure of its sequel: *Latter-day Responsibility.* Individual liberty is but one side of a two-sided coin; you cannot obtain it without its companion, personal responsibility. Thus, my second book outlined a variety of ways that we, both individually and collectively, can increase personal responsibility in order to increase our ability to retain our essential freedoms.

The book was a comparative flop. Its thesis was certainly relevant, but it was definitely not provocative or enticing. It was effectively a list of our shortcomings and how to overcome them. Who likes to be told more things they have to do? We're all busy, we're reasonably content with the status quo in our lives, and we don't need someone coming along to shake things up and give us more homework. The lukewarm reception to *Latter-day Responsibility* taught me that people are understandably less inclined to engage with content that challenges their personal habits or that demands change. It's human nature, after all, to resist anything that disrupts our comfort zones.

Lesson learned. That being said, I want to caution readers that I'm approaching *Rise Up* from this fundamental thesis: we men are operating far beneath our potential and what God expects of us. The scriptural commands to "shake thyself from the dust [and] arise,"[12] or to "awake thou that sleepest,"[13] or to "shake off the chains with which ye are bound"[14]—these

12 Isaiah 52:1-2.
13 Ephesians 5:14.
14 2 Nephi 1:23.

and countless other calls to action in scripture are not gentle suggestions (and yes, they apply equally to women). They are urgent, imperative commands from God, pushing us to break free from complacency and mediocrity. These scriptures, and many others like them, are calls to rise up to the divine potential within us, to shake off the chains of lethargy, sin, and self-doubt that hold us back, and to step into the roles we men were created to fulfill.

We church-goers are used to this, of course; reading scripture and attending worship services expose us to a steady stream of counsel reminding us of our charge and (hopefully) inspiring us to rise to a higher level of discipleship. We know intuitively, as the saying goes, that the Church is not a museum of saints but a hospital for sinners. This phrase derives from an exchange where the Pharisees were aghast at seeing Jesus eat with publicans and sinners. To them, Jesus replied, "They that are whole have no need of the physician, but they that are sick."[15] We sinners are diseased, and we commune together in hopes of improving our spiritual health.

At the risk of going beyond Christ's parable, I wonder if there's a deeper layer to be had. If we see ourselves as sick, we may be tempted to blame external circumstances as we often do with physical illness: "I caught a virus," or "That restaurant undercooked my food." This is a passive approach to perceiving our problematic state. We see it as a temporary condition, typically the fault of others or circumstances beyond our control, which we simply need to wait out. It can lead to passive

15 Mark 2:17.

discipleship: "I'm only human," or "The natural man is hard for anyone to overcome." We excuse our poor decisions and ignore the large distance between us and deity.

What if instead of seeing ourselves as merely sick, we recognize that we are actually dead? Nephi taught that sinners experience a "death of the spirit," noting that "to be carnally-minded is death."[16] Alma said that those who die in a sinful state undergo a "spiritual death" in which they "die as to things pertaining unto righteousness."[17] He taught his son further that Adam and Eve's intentional transgression "brought upon all mankind a spiritual death" in which "they were cut off from the presence of the Lord."[18] And while the fall brought upon us our sinful state, creating a probationary period[19] in order that we might demonstrate faith and obedience to God, it is our own *dis*obedience that perpetuates our separation from Him. Christ's atonement provides an opportunity for "repentance, that ye may not bring down [God's] wrath upon you, that ye may not be bound down by the chains of hell, that ye may not suffer [spiritual] death."[20]

Repentance first begins by baptism—not of sick people, but *dead* ones. Paul taught that we are "baptized into [Jesus Christ's] death," teaching that "Therefore are we buried with him by baptism into death: that like as Christ was raised up from the dead by the glory of the Father, even so we also

16 2 Nephi 9:10, 39.
17 Alma 12:16.
18 Alma 42:9.
19 See Alma 12:24; 42:4, 10; 34:32.
20 Alma 13:30.

should walk in newness of life."[21] This comparison creates contrast—we are dead without Jesus, and only with Him can we obtain "newness of life." As Paul also said, "If any man be in Christ, he is a new creature: old things are passed away; behold, all things are become new."[22] And Mosiah was told by God:

> Marvel not that all mankind, yea, men and women, all nations, kindreds, tongues and people, must be born again; yea, born of God, changed from their carnal and fallen state, to a state of righteousness, being redeemed of God, becoming his sons and daughters; And thus they become new creatures; and unless they do this, they can in nowise inherit the kingdom of God.[23]

Like Neo awaking from the Matrix or Ebenezer Scrooge embracing a new life of generosity and compassion, rising up as men of God requires reframing our entire perspective. It is not linear growth and incremental improvements we need—we must cast aside lesser things, prioritize God's kingdom, and as a brotherhood—a priesthood—fight the night of wrong as we take up our cross.[24] We must think and act like new creatures. We must become alive in the gospel, not sleepily stumbling through minimal checklists of what we perceive it means to be a "temple-worthy Latter-day Saint." It's simply not enough.

---

21 Romans 6:3-4.
22 2 Corinthians 5:17.
23 Mosiah 27:25-26.
24 Matthew 10:38–39, 16:24–25; 3 Nephi 12:30, D&C 23:6.

And why is it not enough? Because scriptural history offers abundant examples of self-described Saints deceiving themselves into wrongfully thinking that they were sufficiently righteous. The children of Israel demanded a king to "be like all the nations," rejecting God while thinking they were still God's people.[25] Throughout the Old Testament, Israelites embraced all manner of idolatry, contently contaminating themselves with the beliefs and actions of surrounding cultures.[26] Some virgins in Jesus' parable who awaited the Bridegroom thought they were prepared but were instead met with His stinging rebuke: "I know you not."[27] Alma encountered the Zoramites, who called themselves "a chosen and a holy people" despite "perverting the ways of the Lord," being "lifted up unto great boasting, in their pride" on the Rameumptom.[28] More recently, Joseph Smith observed:

> I have tried for a number of years to get the minds of the Saints prepared to receive the things of God; but we frequently see some of them, after suffering all they have for the work of God, will fly to pieces like glass as soon as anything comes that is contrary to their traditions: they cannot stand the fire at all. How many will be able to abide a celestial law, and go through and receive their exaltation, I am unable to say, as many are called, but few are chosen.[29]

---

25 1 Samuel 8:5-7.

26 See Exodus 32:1-4; Judges 2:11-13; 1 Kings 11:4-8; 2 Kings 17:7-12; Jeremiah 2:11-13; Ezekiel 20:32.

27 Matthew 25:1-12.

28 Alma 31.

29 *History of the Church*, 6:184–85; from a discourse given by Joseph Smith on Jan. 21, 1844, in Nauvoo, Illinois.

I imagine some subset of this book's readers—but surely not *you*—might have a similar mindset. After all, aren't we God's chosen people as long as we're baptized, paying our tithing, going to church, and being nice to others? Sure, we're all a little sick—due to the contagious environment we're in—but surely we're not spiritually *dead*, right? The reality should be painfully clear: we Latter-day Saints are not immune to this historical trend and, as I will make clear later in the book, I think, in many ways, we're in a worse position.[30]

As I review the state of men today—in the Church and throughout society—I cannot help but observe that we are falling into these same self-delusions. Many of us who obediently sit in the pews each week still "take on the slow stain of the world," as President Gordon B. Hinckley once said.[31] We think we reside in and are building Zion, while too many of us, as Elder Neal A. Maxwell quipped, have a "summer cottage in Babylon"[32] that we regularly frequent. Despite our awareness of the scripture in a superficial sense, we actively try to serve two masters.[33] Due to his prophetic calling and visions, Lehi was no doubt aware of these trends and the propensity with which God's people draw near to Him with their lips (or, their words) while their hearts are far from Him.[34] As he lay

---

30 For an expanded treatment of this topic, see Connor Boyack, *The Slow Stain: Lessons from the Past, Warnings for Today* (Lehi: Social Harmony, 2025).

31 Gordon B. Hinckley, "Stand Strong against the Wiles of the World," *Ensign* (November 1995), 98.

32 Neal A. Maxwell, *A Wonderful Flood of Light* (Salt Lake City: Deseret Book, 1990), 47.

33 Matthew 6:24.

34 Matthew 15:8-9.

on his deathbed, Lehi called his children to action, much like Merrill's lyrics do:

> O that ye would awake; awake from a deep sleep, yea, even from the sleep of hell, and shake off the awful chains by which ye are bound, which are the chains which bind the children of men, that they are carried away captive down to the eternal gulf of misery and woe. Awake! and arise from the dust...[35]

My purpose in writing this book is to help make convincingly clear how guilty we are of being asleep and provide suggestions and ideas for how we might awake and arise—how we, as men of God, can rise up and build Zion in these latter days. Together, we will explore how to break free from complacency and rise to the challenge of becoming the men God intended us to be.

35 2 Nephi 1:13-14.

INTRODUCTION

As the COVID-19 pandemic spread across the globe, a compliant media quickly helped build the case for compulsory masking. Nearly 80 percent of opinion articles published by corporate media outlets advocated for wearing masks, whereas fewer than 3 percent opposed.[1] The Associated Press claimed that "Not wearing a mask during [the] COVID-19 health emergency isn't a free speech right."[2] CNN published an article calling those not wearing masks "A group of people whining so much over something so little."[3] MSNBC's Nicole Wallace said on air that it was "pathetic" that President Trump didn't wear a mask for the first several months of the pandemic.[4] When one mask wasn't working, *The Guardian*

---

1 Scoville, C., McCumber, A., Amironesei, R., & Jeon, J., "Mask Refusal Backlash: The Politicization of Face Masks in the American Public Sphere during the Early Stages of the COVID-19 Pandemic," *Socius* (2022), 8.

2 "Not wearing a mask during COVID-19 health emergency isn't a free speech right, appeals court says," The Associated Press, February 6, 2024, https://apnews.com/article/covid-mask-free-speech-lawsuits-new-jersey-108abf877288999f34d-1c604b731d34c.

3 "Anti-maskers: A group of people whining so much over something so little," CNN, November 13, 2020, https://www.cnn.com/2020/11/13/opinions/utah-covid-cases-anti-maskers-austin/index.html.

4 "Nicole Wallace: 'Pathetic' that it took Trump 5 months to finally wear a mask," MSNBC, July 21, 2020, https://www.msnbc.com/msnbc/watch/nicole-wallace-pathetic-that-it-took-

obediently reported that a "CDC study recommends double masking to reduce COVID-19 exposure."[5]

The media's relentless campaign was not, however, a solo project. The chorus of voices included celebrities, government officials, dancing nurses on TikTok, pastors, and more. Police officers targeted noncompliant offenders, removing them from playing at the beach,[6] worshipping in a religious service,[7] or physically dragging them off a bus.[8] Arnold Schwarzenegger told those not wearing masks, "Screw your freedom!"[9] Later, he wrote an article for *The Atlantic* titled, "Don't Be a Schmuck. Put on a Mask."[10] Jennifer Aniston posted a selfie showing her wearing a mask, including the hashtag #wearadamnmask in the caption.[11] Mark Hamill, who played

---

trump-5-months-to-finally-wear-a-mask-88083525565.

5 "CDC study recommends double masking to reduce Covid-19 exposure," *The Guardian*, February 10, 2021, https://www.theguardian.com/world/2021/feb/10/mask-guidance-cdc-two-masks-close-fitting.

6 "Hundreds arrested in Miami Beach as spring breakers ignore COVID-19 protocols, mayor says," CBS, March 16, 2021, https://www.cbsnews.com/news/spring-break-miami-beach-covid-19-protocols-hundreds-arrested/.

7 "3 arrested at Idaho church singing event to flout mask order," The Associated Press, September 24, 2020, https://apnews.com/general-news-493cfd970eda54a57b8bc6ebb7f5d5f2.

8 "Philly Police Drag Man From Bus for Not Wearing a Face Mask," *New York Magazine*, April 10, 2020, https://nymag.com/intelligencer/2020/04/philly-police-drag-man-from-bus-for-not-wearing-a-face-mask.html.

9 "Arnold Schwarzenegger rips anti-maskers: 'Screw your freedom'," *New York Post*, August 12, 2021, https://nypost.com/2021/08/12/arnold-schwarzenegger-on-anti-maskers-screw-your-freedom/.

10 "Don't Be a Schmuck. Put on a Mask.," *The Atlantic*, August 13, 2021, https://www.theatlantic.com/ideas/archive/2021/08/schwarzenegger-schmuck-mask-vaccines/619746/.

11 "Hollywood speaks out: 10 celebrities say wear your mask,"

Luke Skywalker in *Star Wars*, threw out a caption of his own: #RealMenWearMasks.[12] Tom Hanks said, "Shame on you" to anyone not wearing a mask.[13]

Yet despite the onslaught of opinion and peer pressure, many still resisted—especially men. The BBC, peering from across the pond, wondered, "Why is there a US backlash to masks?"[14] Just a few years prior, a study found that men are "less likely than women to adopt protective behaviors, like... wearing masks"[15]—and in the years since, three additional studies have arrived at the same conclusion.[16] "Masculine toughness is consistently related to higher negative feelings and lower positive feelings about mask wearing," noted the authors of one of the studies.[17] The title of the study was indicative of the thesis its authors were evangelizing: "Toxic

---

Gulf News, July 2, 2020, https://gulfnews.com/photos/entertainment/hollywood-speaks-out-10-celebrities-say-wear-your-mask-1.1593692928676?slide=1.

12 Ibid.

13 Ibid.

14 "Coronavirus: Why is there a US backlash to masks?," BBC, may 5, 2020, https://www.bbc.com/news/world-us-canada-52540015.

15 Kelly R. Moran and Sara Y Del Valle, "A Meta-Analysis of the Association between Gender and Protective Behaviors in Response to Respiratory Epidemics and Pandemics," PloS one vol. 11,10 e0164541, 21 Oct. 2016.

16 See Dan Cassino, and Yasemin Besen-Cassino, "Of Masks and Men? Gender, Sex, and Protective Measures during COVID-19," *Politics & Gender* 16, no. 4 (2020), 1052–62; Tyler T. Reny, "Masculine Norms and Infectious Disease: The Case of COVID-19," *Politics & Gender* 16, no. 4 (2020), 1028–35; Carl L. Palmer and Rolfe D. Peterson, "Toxic Mask-Ulinity: The Link between Masculine Toughness and Affective Reactions to Mask Wearing in the COVID-19 Era," *Politics & Gender* 16, no. 4 (2020), 1044–51.

17 Ibid.

Mask-Ulinity: The Link between Masculine Toughness and Affective Reactions to Mask Wearing in the COVID-19 Era." Why the predominantly male resistance to mask compliance? It seems that the chorus of voices across academia, entertainment, media, and politics was settling upon the same answer as this study's authors: "toxic masculinity."

For example, a headline from *The New York Times* told its readers, "How an Aversion to Masks Stems from Toxic Masculinity."[18] But masks were not the sole focus of those who employed this term to denigrate men. It was invoked by Gilette in a viral advertisement depicting boys bullying other boys, women being harassed and cat-called, and a group of men excusing all of it as part of the male experience.[19] And just days before the release of the ad, the American Psychological Association issued new "Guidelines for the Psychological Practice with Boys and Men," warning that "traditional" masculine traits are linked to aggression and negative health outcomes. The guide defines "traditional masculinity" as "a particular constellation of standards that have held sway over large segments of the population, including: anti-femininity, achievement, eschewal of the appearance of weakness, and adventure, risk, and violence."[20] The organization's summa-

18 "How an Aversion to Masks Stems From 'Toxic Masculinity'," *The New York Times*, October 22, 2020, https://www.nytimes.com/2020/10/22/us/masks-toxic-masculinity-covid-men-gender.html.

19 "Reactions to Gillette Ad Prove Toxic Masculinity Is Real," Bazaar, January 18, 2019, https://www.harpersbazaar.com/culture/politics/a25934344/gillette-ad-controversy-toxic-masculinity-explained/.

20 "APA Guidelines for Psychological Practice with Boys and Men," American Psychological Association, August 2018,

ry of their guidelines states that "Traditional masculinity—marked by stoicism, competitiveness, dominance and aggression—is, on the whole, harmful."[21]

Toxic masculinity has been blamed for rape,[22] murder,[23] mass shootings,[24] gang violence,[25] online trolling,[26] climate change,[27] the United Kingdom leaving the European Union,[28]

---

https://www.apa.org/about/policy/boys-men-practice-guidelines.pdf.

21 "APA issues first-ever guidelines for practice with men and boys," The American Psychological Association, January 2019, https://www.apa.org/monitor/2019/01/ce-corner.

22 "Science Says Toxic Masculinity — More Than Alcohol — Leads To Sexual Assault," FiveThirtyEight, September 26, 2018, https://fivethirtyeight.com/features/science-says-toxic-masculinity-more-than-alcohol-leads-to-sexual-assault/.

23 "The Mollie Tibbetts killing is not about immigration, it's about toxic masculinity," Yahoo!, August 23, 2018, https://www.yahoo.com/lifestyle/mollie-tibbetts-murder-not-immigration-toxic-masculinity-213805650.html.

24 "Overcompensation Nation: It's time to admit that toxic masculinity drives gun violence," Salon, June 13, 2016, https://www.salon.com/2016/06/13/overcompensation_nation_its_time_to_admit_that_toxic_masculinity_drives_gun_violence/.

25 "How men at New Folsom Prison reckon with toxic masculinity," *Los Angeles Times*, November 30, 2017, https://www.latimes.com/opinion/op-ed/la-oe-jackson-men-group-therapy-folsom-prison-the-work-toxic-masculinity-20171130-story.html.

26 "Woke Daddy: The feminist dad challenging toxic masculinity and facing right-wing abuse," *The Independent*, June 20, 2017, https://www.independent.co.uk/life-style/woke-daddy-feminist-dad-toxic-masculinity-online-trolls-rightwing-abuse-ludo-gabriele-blog-a7798576.html.

27 "Toxic masculinity is literally bad for the planet, according to research," *The Sydney Morning Herald*, September 1, 2016, https://www.smh.com.au/lifestyle/how-getting-in-touch-with-your-feminine-side-might-save-the-planet-20160901-gr68oy.html.

28 "The Brexiteers represent the four faces of toxic masculinity," The New Statesman, July 5, 2018, https://www.newstatesman.com/politics/2018/07/brexiteers-represent-four-faces-toxic-masculinity.

and the election of Donald Trump.[29] And while the term is used generously and frequently by feminist critics of gender norms, that's not where it originated; it was coined in the 1980s by a men's movement *reacting* to second-wave feminism. These men held workshops and wilderness retreats for men to promote masculine spirituality and "rescue what it referred to as the 'deep masculine'—a protectively, 'warrior' masculinity—from toxic masculinity."[30] The problem many were seeing in men, according to this movement, was the toxicity derived from feminizing boys and removing the rites and rituals from society that lead boys to become men. So while the term is used differently today than when it began, it seems everyone can agree that there's something amiss with manhood in modern society.

Before we delve into how to rise up as men, it would be helpful to survey the landscape in a bit more detail to understand what we're dealing with. Before addressing some of the concerning psychological and physical challenges men are facing, let's review the perception that's been created about them. Throughout the entertainment industry, men are portrayed as lazy, incompetent, and stupid—they're the punching bag for jokes, and another child for mom to manage. Al Bundy in *Married With Children*, Homer Simpson in *The Simpsons*, Hal Wilkerson in *Malcolm in the Middle*, Peter Griffin in *Fam-*

---

29 "Donald Trump's Toxic Masculinity," *The New York Times*, October 13, 2016, https://www.nytimes.com/2016/10/13/opinion/donald-trumps-toxic-masculinity.html.

30 "The Problem With a Fight Against Toxic Masculinity," *The Atlantic*, February 27, 2019, https://www.theatlantic.com/health/archive/2019/02/toxic-masculinity-history/583411/.

ily Guy, Ray Barone in *Everybody Loves Raymond*, Daddy Pig in *Peppa Pig*, Phil Dunphy in *Modern Family*, and a whole host of recent kids' cartoons and family entertainment all reinforce the stereotype. Sure, it's humorous to watch a bumbling Fred Flintstone foul things up for the family, but when the occasional character becomes a persistent stereotype reinforced across various media and over a long period of time, one can reasonably expect the message to stick and alter men's perceptions about themselves in society. Negative portrayals of fathers and husbands in modern media create the impression among viewers that men need not assume these roles because clearly they're neither important nor helpful. Doofus dads and idiot husbands are role models whether we like it or not. When Huggies created a commercial in 2012 for their diapers, they told viewers that, to prove the diapers can handle just about anything, "We put them to the toughest test imaginable: dads, alone with their babies, in one house, for five days."[31] Reinforcing a stereotype about men as incompetent caregivers moves from fiction to reality as millions of consumers passively ingest this message over and over again throughout their lives.

If you tell men they're not needed—or worse, that they're an annoyance—then perhaps they'll believe you and abandon their role as father and husband. In 1960, 17.5 percent of children lived apart from their fathers.[32] Today, that number has

31 "Huggies Pulls Ridiculous Ads After Dads Portrayed As Idiots," Mommyish, March 15, 2012, https://mommyish.com/huggies-pulls-ads-after-dads-portrayed-as-idiots-134/.

32 David Blakenhorn, *Fatherless America: Confronting Our Most Urgent Social Problem* (New York: HarperCollins, 1995),

surged to over one-third of all children—over 25 million kids growing up without their biological father.[33] And while there are clearly justifiable exceptions to maintaining a two-parent household—as in the case of abuse, abandonment, or an affair—what's clear is that the exception has transformed into a trend. This alarming absenteeism of fathers contributes to a cascade of downstream social degeneracy: fatherless children experience poverty at four times the rate of kids with married parents;[34] children without a present father are far more likely to abuse drugs and alcohol;[35] fatherless daughters are four times more likely to get pregnant as teenagers;[36] and kids raised in families without a father are more than twice as likely to commit suicide.[37] Dozens more data points help make the conclusion clear: as we push fathers to the margins,

---

18–19.

33 U.S. Census Bureau, Current Population Survey, "Living Arrangements of Children under 18 Years/1 and Marital Status of Parents by Age, Sex, Race, and Hispanic Origin/2 and Selected Characteristics of the Child for all Children 2010," Table C3, November, 2010.

34 U.S. Department of Health and Human Services, "ASEP Issue Brief: Information on Poverty and Income Statistics," September 12, 2012 http://aspe.hhs.gov/hsp/12/PovertyAndIncomeEst/ib.shtml.

35 John Hoffmann, "The Community Context of Family Structure and Adolescent Drug Use," *Journal of Marriage and Family* 64 (May 2002), 314-330.

36 J.D. Teachman, "The Childhood Living Arrangements of Children and the Characteristics of Their Marriages," *Journal of Family Issues*, 25(1), 86-111, https://doi.org/10.1177/0192513X03255346.

37 "Absent Parent Doubles Child Suicide Risk," WebMD, January 23, 2003, http://www.webmd.com/baby/news/20030123/absent-parent-doubles-child-suicide-risk.

we unwittingly unravel the very fabric of society, leaving our children to bear the burden of a broken legacy.

Millions more children are fortunate to have a father who is physically present, yet in many cases, he is emotionally absent. An intact family is not necessarily a strong family; one can shirk one's duties while still eating meals and sleeping in the family home. Disengagement can result from a variety of circumstances, including basic mental health challenges. Men, after all, are four times more likely to commit suicide than women[38]—and 15 percent of men say they have no close friends, up from 3 percent in 1990.[39] As the traditional providers, men face increasing pressure in an inflationary environment, causing financial strain on the family—a leading cause of divorce.[40] No one questioned the Simpson family living in a decent home on a single salary earned by a factory worker without a college degree. Yet today, many men struggle to earn enough to keep their family comfortable, often working two jobs or juggling side hustles to stay afloat. Their wages today, adjusted for inflation, are lower than they were in 1979—while the cost of living surges all around them.[41]

---

38 "Why the Men's Suicide Rate Is So High," Healthline, August 4, 2023, https://www.healthline.com/health/mens-health/mens-suicide-rate.

39 "Men's Social Circles are Shrinking," AEI, June 29, 2021, https://www.americansurveycenter.org/why-mens-social-circles-are-shrinking/.

40 "Leading Causes Of Divorce: 43% Report Lack Of Family Support," Forbes, August 15, 2023, https://www.forbes.com/advisor/legal/divorce/common-causes-divorce/.

41 Sarah Donovan and David Bradley, *Real Wage Trends, 1979 to 2019* (Washington, DC: Congressional Research Service, 2020).

They're overworked, depressed, fatigued, and often not supported or mentally cared for, told instead to "tough it out." When fathers are disengaged—distracted by work, personal interests, or the overwhelming pressures of modern life—they miss the opportunity to forge deep, meaningful connections with their children. These connections are crucial for a child's development, influencing their self-esteem, emotional well-being, and ability to form healthy relationships in the future. And while it's good that these men have not abandoned their families physically, emotional abandonment can be just as bad—and sometimes worse.

The list of male woes could fill this entire book, so let's speed through a few final ones and then get down to rising up. Here's something alarming: sperm counts are dropping. It's "Spermageddon" according to one meta-analysis of 223 research studies published between 1873 and 2018. The survey of this data, involving a combined 57,000 men across 53 countries, found that in the last half a century, total sperm counts dropped by 62.3 percent.[42] Testosterone is following a similar trend. The most prominent study on the topic revealed a "substantial" drop in the testosterone levels of men in the US since the 1980s, with a 1 percent drop each year. "This means," a reporter observed, "that a 65-year-old man in 2002 would have testosterone levels 15 percent lower than those of a 65-year-old in 1987."[43] The "alarming" trend, as one research team

42 "Human Sperm Counts Declining Worldwide, Study Finds," *Smithsonian Magazine*, November 22, 2022, https://www.smithsonianmag.com/smart-news/human-sperm-counts-declining-worldwide-study-finds-180981138/.

43 "Men's testosterone levels declined in last 20 years," Reuters,

rightly called it,[44] is not a result of an aging population; across all ages of men, the male hormone is on the decline.

Men are 22 percent more likely to abuse illicit substances than women,[45] and are three times more likely to regularly consume pornography.[46] Boys are at least twice as likely to be diagnosed with ADHD as girls and twice as likely to be suspended;[47] school dropout rates for boys are much higher than girls.[48] Take the top 10 percent of a freshman high school class, and only one-third will be boys.[49] Girls get better grades and graduate at higher rates.[50] All of this contributes to what has been called "the male drift," in which young men develop a deep-seated apathy about education, employment, personal health, marriage, and life in general. Contrib-

---

August 9, 2007, https://www.reuters.com/article/health-testosterone-levels-dc-idUKKIM16976320061101/?edition-redirect=uk.

44 Anna-Maria Andersson, Tina K. Jensen, Anders Juul, Jørgen H. Petersen, Torben Jørgensen, Niels E. Skakkebæk, "Secular Decline in Male Testosterone and Sex Hormone Binding Globulin Serum Levels in Danish Population Surveys," *The Journal of Clinical Endocrinology & Metabolism*, Volume 92, Issue 12, December 1 2007, Pages 4696–4705, https://doi.org/10.1210/jc.2006-2633.

45 Center for Behavioral Health Statistics and Quality, Results from the 2016 National Survey on Drug Use and Health: Detailed Tables. Rockville, MD: Substance Abuse and Mental Health Services Administration; 2017.

46 "Porn Addiction," Psychology Today, accessed August 28, 2024, https://www.psychologytoday.com/us/basics/porn-addiction.

47 "What's the Matter with Men?," *The New Yorker*, January 23, 2023, https://www.newyorker.com/magazine/2023/01/30/whats-the-matter-with-men.

48 Ibid.

49 Ibid.

50 "How the Schools Shortchange Boys," *City Journal*, Summer 2006, https://www.city-journal.org/article/how-the-schools-shortchange-boys.

uting to this trend is the lack of nonfamilial male role models; children who spend most of their productive hours during their most formative years of development in a school environment are primarily exposed to adult women, not men. In the United States, more than three-quarters of teachers are women,[51] up from 67 percent in 1980;[52] in elementary school specifically, women constitute more than 90 percent of the teaching force.[53] The imbalance is a downstream result of over 80 percent of Bachelor's degrees in Education being earned by women.[54] There's nothing wrong, of course, with women teaching—but when children, especially boys, lack positive male role models in their lives, a vicious cycle spirals society downward.

Another aspect of the male drift is the disruption to the labor force that jeopardizes the success of their primary role as providers. In the US, labor force participation among men has dropped seven percentage points over the last half-century, from 96 to 89 percent.[55] Young men aged 25–34 have seen the

---

51 "Still Mostly White and Female: New Federal Data on the Teaching Profession," EdWeek, April 14, 2020, https://www.edweek.org/leadership/still-mostly-white-and-female-new-federal-data-on-the-teaching-profession/2020/04.

52 Richard M. Ingersoll, "Seven Trends: The Transformation of the Teaching Force—Updated October 2018," University of Pennsylvania, CPRE Research Reports, 2018.

53 "The U.S. Teaching Population Is Getting Bigger, and More Female," *The Atlantic*, February 20, 2019, https://www.theatlantic.com/education/archive/2019/02/the-explosion-of-women-teachers/582622/.

54 "Why are So Many Teachers Women?," National Women's History Museum, August 17, 2017, https://www.womenshistory.org/articles/why-are-so-many-teachers-women.

55 U.S. Bureau of Labor Statistics, Series ID: LNS11300061Q.

steepest drop, as the proportion not even looking for work has doubled since 1980.[56] The economy's transition from manufacturing to a service-based economy, in addition to the heavy outsourcing of remaining manufacturing jobs, has reduced the economic opportunity for men; service-based jobs are much more accessible to women, as they require emotional intelligence and communication skills.[57] And with the advent of automation and artificial intelligence, men's traditional roles face further decline, as one scholar wrote:

> The occupations most susceptible to automation are... more likely to employ men, as my colleague Mark Muro shows. "Men... make up over 70 percent of production occupations, over 80 percent of transportation occupations, and over 90 percent of construction and installation occupations," he writes. And these are "all occupational groups with current task loads that have above-average projected automation exposure." By contrast, women make up most of the workforce in relatively automation-safe occupations such as health care, personal services, and education.[58]

---

56 Richard Reeves and Eleanor Krause, "Why Are Young, Educated Men Working Less?," Brookings Institute, February 23, 2018; see also Grant Bailey and Bradley Wilcox, "Out of Work and On the Dole: Is Uncle Sam Contributing to Young Men's Malaise?" Institute for Family Studies, May 14, 2025, https://ifstudies.org/blog/out-of-work-and-on-the-dole-is-uncle-sam-contributing-to-young-mens-malaise.

57 See Daniel Bell, *The Coming Of Post-Industrial Society* (New York: Basic Books, 1976).

58 Richard V. Reeves, *Of Boys and Men: Why the Modern Male Is Struggling, Why It Matters, and What To Do About It* (Washington, DC: Brookings Institution Press, 2022), 21.

This educational and economic disparity is clearly evident in the data. Here's a quick peek at just part of the gender imbalance:[59]

For every 100 girls/women...	There are _____ boys/men...
Who earn an associate's degree	63
Enrolled in US graduate schools	73
Who earn a bachelor's degree	74
Whose entry into kindergarten is delayed	139
Who are homeless	154
Who abuse illicit drugs and alcohol	180
In K-12 with a learning disability	207
Twenty-five to 34-year-olds who die	232
Ages 20 to 29 who commit suicide	450

59 "Chart of the Day: For Every 100 Girls/women.....," American Enterprise Institute, December 23, 2019, https://www.aei.org/carpe-diem/chart-of-the-day-for-every-100-girls-women/.

For every 100 girls/women...	There are _____ boys/men...
Under age 18 who are in a correctional facility	770
Who die on the job	1,294
In a federal prison	1,333

Toxic or otherwise, masculinity is not doing great. How can men dig out of these holes if they are taught the perceived perils of manhood far more often than its virtues and importance? When writer Peggy Orenstein was conducting research for a book about boys, few of the young men she interviewed had an answer to give her when she asked them what they liked about being a boy. "That's interesting," one college sophomore told her. "I never really thought about that. You hear a lot more about what is *wrong* with guys."[60] Is it any wonder that after being told for years that they and their masculinity are the problem, more and more men are retreating into idleness, pornography, and video games? The male drift makes sense in the context of the recent and repeated emphasis on "toxic masculinity." And that message has left a mark—according to one survey, over half of men in the US now believe that society "punishes men just for acting like men."[61]

---

60 Peggy Orenstein, "The Miseducation of the American Boy," *The Atlantic*, January 2020, https://www.theatlantic.com/magazine/archive/2020/01/the-miseducation-of-the-american-boy/603046/.

61 "Dueling Realities: Amid Multiple Crises, Trump and Biden

—w—

This is only a little of what men are up against—economic evolution that displaces them, cultural attitudes that demean them, political plans that ignore them, and social systems that fail to support them. L. Tom Perry observed what we've already reviewed—that today's media "have been relentless in their attacks—ridiculing and demeaning husbands and fathers in their God-given roles," putting men in "the crosshairs of Satan's scope."[62] And as then-Elder James E. Faust pointed out, much of the criticism comes from those who operate in a fixed-sum mindset: "There are some voices in our society who would demean some of the attributes of masculinity. A few of these are women who mistakenly believe that they build their own feminine causes by tearing down the image of manhood."[63] But the reality is that, despite these headwinds, God appointed certain roles to men and expects us to fill those roles honorably. "By divine design," the well-known Proclamation reads, "fathers are to preside over their families in love and righteousness and are responsible to provide the necessities of life and protection for their families."[64] And as fathers, we must model for our boys what being men of God

---

Supporters See Different Priorities and Futures for the Nation," PRRI, October 19, 2020.

62 L. Tom Perry, "Fatherhood, an Eternal Calling," General Conference, April 2004.

63 James E. Faust, "Happiness Is Having a Father Who Cares," General Conference, October 1973.

64 "The Family Proclamation," The Church of Jesus Christ of Latter-day Saints, https://www.churchofjesuschrist.org/study/scriptures/the-family-a-proclamation-to-the-world/the-family-a-proclamation-to-the-world.

looks like. "Boys need men to learn from," Marion D. Hanks taught, "men to be with who understand their need for activities that are challenging and socially and spiritually constructive and that stretch them and give them a chance to learn manly skills, men to love and who love them, men who are models of what a man ought to be."[65]

Perhaps it is true, as psychologist Jordan Peterson argued, that "The West has lost faith in masculinity."[66] Everywhere around us, it appears under siege. Too many men have responded not by rounding their shoulders and rising to the occasion, but by drifting alongside social currents and becoming beta males, ever-apologetic for their masculinity. They have adopted a posture of passivity, apologizing for traits once seen as virtues: strength, assertiveness, and leadership. Instead of pushing back against the tide of cultural critique, many men have internalized the message that their very nature is a problem to be managed rather than a force for good to be harnessed. This crisis of confidence has left a vacuum where true masculinity should thrive—men capable of standing firm, taking responsibility, and leading with conviction. And in that vacuum are men who are disengaged, directionless, and easily swayed by the whims of a society that no longer values their contributions. In many cases, the once-celebrated archetype of the strong, stoic provider has been replaced by men who either reject their masculine identity entirely or, worse, ac-

65 Marion D. Hanks, "Boys Need Men," General Conference, April 1974.

66 "The West Has Lost Faith In Masculinity," Bite-sized Philosophy, YouTube, accessed October 13, 2024, https://www.youtube.com/watch?v=iNlQVMCG-eo.

cept the diminished and caricatured version of it that modern culture offers. Instead of fulfilling their natural roles to provide, protect, and even preside, many men have chosen to abdicate these responsibilities, resulting in broken homes, fractured communities, and a pervasive sense of purposelessness among young men.

This retreat must be reversed. More so than in William Merrill's day, men today—especially men of God who act with persuasion, long-suffering, gentleness, and meekness[67]—must rise up and do their duty. "Let every man learn his duty," the Lord said, for "he that is slothful shall not be counted worthy to stand."[68] Our Church, our communities, and our future need men of God to stand; "men should be anxiously engaged in a good cause, and do many things of their own free will, and bring to pass much righteousness."[69] Heaven knows that the world needs this desperately.

Merrill's lyrics provide a useful foundation upon which to build the case for men of God to rise up and do great things. Thus, the first chapter in this book will address the lesser things that besiege us today, since in order to rise up, we must understand how we are kept down. What are the forces, spiritual and otherwise, that distract us from our mission? What temptations beguile men into spending their time and energy in frivolous or destructive ways? What cultural trends trap us with flaxen cords,[70] giving the appearance of freedom while

---

67 D&C 121:41.
68 D&C 107:99–100.
69 D&C 58:27.
70 2 Nephi 26:22.

subtly seducing us into servitude to Satan and his many minions? These and other questions will offer us the opportunity to take an honest assessment of how well we are doing and whether we've become part of the group Nephi warned of in our day:

> And others will he pacify, and lull them away into carnal security, that they will say: All is well in Zion; yea, Zion prospereth, all is well—and thus the devil cheateth their souls, and leadeth them away carefully down to hell.[71]

Merrill next calls on men of God to give their heart and mind and soul and strength to serve Him. Though it's the second chapter in the book, it's the first commandment, emphasized by Jesus to His disciples: "And thou shalt love the Lord thy God with all thy heart, and with all thy soul, and with all thy mind, and with all thy strength."[72] But what does this mean in practical terms? We all claim to love God, and yet He continually rebukes people for giving lip service in lieu of actually giving their heart and mind and soul and strength to Him. "This people draweth nigh unto me with their mouth, and honoureth me with their lips," He said in the Old Testament, the New Testament, and to Joseph Smith in the modern era. "But their heart is far from me."[73] How do we not act like foolish virgins, going through outward motions without doing what's actually necessary to give our all to God?[74] What does

---

71 2 Nephi 28:21.

72 Mark 12:30.

73 Matthew 15:8; Isaiah 29:13; Joseph Smith—History 1:19.

74 Matthew 25:1-13.

such fidelity to the Lord look like in our secular age? Provocative questions lead to powerful answers, which we'll tackle together shortly.

The third chapter focuses on how difficult it is to remain consistently faithful since the "kingdom tarries long." The virgins waited a while, and in that prolonged period, it can be easy to relax our religiosity and become derelict in our duties. How do we guard against distractions that vie for our attention while we wait on the Lord? The answer lies in cultivating a deliberate discipleship that permeates our life. To love God with all our heart, mind, soul, and strength requires more than routine participation in Sunday services; it demands an inner transformation, a realignment of priorities, and a willingness to sacrifice. We'll explore how to nurture this depth of commitment even when the urgency of our faith seems to fade in the everyday busyness of life.

Just as Merrill and his Presbyterian peers united in a brotherhood to respond to the concerns of their day, so too must we. Chapter Four shares a vision for this "day of brotherhood" and what the priesthood's potential could be if we collectively responded to God's call. The revised version in the Church's hymnal refers to this brotherhood as "one united throng," but in a polarized society where our disagreements are amplified above our agreements, how do we unite together as men of God? The answer might lie in the past: early Saints had their own internal conflicts and cultural corruption to deal with, yet many of them pressed forward because they were united by a vision larger than themselves—the building of Zion. The ideal of a modern-day Zion requires us to forge bonds of brotherhood so the priesthood's power can become an unstoppable force for good in the world. Men adrift at spiritual sea are slothful servants whose spiritual energy is wasted. Only by uniting in purpose can we harness the priesthood's power to build Zion and fulfill God's work.

Chapter Five contrasts this bright day of brotherhood against the dark night of wrong. What things lie in the darkness that impede our work? We're commanded to "waste and wear out our lives in bringing to light all the hidden things of darkness,"[75] but what are they exactly? God wants these nefarious deeds "made manifest in the light,"[76] but too many men are ignorant of the dark forces operating around us—a continuation of the War in Heaven that is producing countless spiritual casualties today. A brotherhood united *for* something implicitly unites *against* its opposite; as we cultivate the light of Christ in our lives, we can use it to fight against Satan's dark operations. Doing so successfully, though, requires that we be aware of what this darkness is and where it exists.

In Chapter Six, we review the omitted verse from Merrill's original and consider why the Church may not have wanted Saints singing about how "the church for you doth wait." We will review both institutional obligations—things the Church is tasked with doing collectively—and individual ones. Are we to build the kingdom of God independently or only under the direction of the Church's organizational structure? Do we defer to Church leaders and await their counsel for what we ought to do, or should we act of our own accord? Are we cogs

75 D&C 123:13.
76 2 Nephi 30:17.

in a Church machine or independent operators tasked with advancing God's kingdom in our own spheres of influence? These are critical questions that cut to the heart of what it means to be a disciple in the modern Church. In this chapter, we'll explore the tension between institutional loyalty and individual initiative—and why the Church's "strength [might be] unequal to her task."

Finally, we'll explore what it means to "tread where [Christ's] feet have trod." Jesus's teachings were often countercultural—in other words, in opposition to the prevailing cultural trends and norms of the day—and they remain so in our modern era. What does it look like, then, to be a true disciple of Christ in a secular society that has accepted a diluted, impotent version of Christianity? Following Christ's path—and taking up our cross—means to embrace a path that is often uncomfortable, challenging, and at odds with the world's expectations. Christ did not seek popularity, nor did He conform to societal pressures; rather, He boldly spoke truth, even (and especially) when it was unpopular or dangerous. In a secular society that promotes convenience, materialism, and moral relativism, being a true disciple requires more than passive belief—it demands action, courage, and a willingness to stand apart. Are we content with a comfortable Christianity that blends into the cultural fabric, or are we prepared to be the "peculiar people" that Christ calls us to be?

The state of modern masculinity is grim, and yet, amid the chaos, there lies a powerful opportunity. In the face of societal decline, where men are ridiculed, diminished, and driven to the margins, the call to rise up has never been more urgent.

We've reviewed some of the immense cultural forces working against men—from the media's mockery of fatherhood to the alarming data on absent fathers and declining masculine virtue. But the true message here is not one of despair—it's a rallying cry. The world may be losing faith in men, but men of faith must now rise and reclaim their God-given roles with strength, purpose, and conviction. The battle lines are drawn, and it's time for men to step up and fight.

LESSER THINGS

How might men, who are called by God to rise up, instead be kept down? That is the question C.S. Lewis tackled in his allegorical work, *The Screwtape Letters*—a book that explores the subtle tactics used by spiritual forces to lead men astray. Through the letters of Screwtape, a senior demon mentoring his apprentice, Wormwood, Lewis illustrates that the most effective method of damnation isn't always through grand temptations or overt acts of evil. Instead, it is the slow, steady drift into complacency and mediocrity that ensnares men. "Indeed, the safest road to Hell is the gradual one," Screwtape wrote. "The gentle slope, soft underfoot, without sudden turnings, without milestones, without signposts."[1]

This deliberate strategy of distraction and seduction mirrors the challenges men face today, as they are besieged by minor diversions—lesser things—that slowly pull them away from their higher purpose. At face value, their minor status means that the individual can continue seeing themselves as sufficiently righteous overall, despite a few flaws here and there. But like a chink in one's armor, that minor vulnerability can lead to a fatal weakness that provides the enemy an opportunity to attack. Lewis has Screwtape explain that it is not

1 C.S. Lewis, *The Complete C.S. Lewis Signature Classics* (New York: HarperCollins Publishers, 2002), 220.

the magnitude of the sin that matters, but the cumulative effect of small distractions and indulgences that create distance between man and his divine purpose:

> You will say that these are very small sins, and doubtless, like all young tempters, you are anxious to be able to report spectacular wickedness. But do remember, the only thing that matters is the extent to which you separate the man from the Enemy. It does not matter how small the sins are, provided that their cumulative effect is to edge the man away from the Light and out into the Nothing.[2]

Over and over again throughout scripture, God's chosen people succumbed to the Screwtapes and Wormwoods of their day, prioritizing lesser things that pulled them away from God's path. Like all flaxen cords, at first they appear light and harmless, only to tighten over time, binding men in ways they may not fully recognize until it's too late. The children of Israel's restlessness and frustration exploded into full-blown idolatry.[3] The Nephites, after periods of prosperity, consistently fell into pride and wickedness, shifting their focus from gratitude and humility to pride, wealth, and power.[4] Samson's incredible strength was undermined as a result of his pursuit of the Philistine woman Delilah.[5] Similarly, the great Solomon allowed his love for foreign women—who the Jews had been forbidden to marry—to lead him (and through

---

2 Ibid.

3 Exodus 32.

4 Alma 4:6–8; Helaman 6:17; 12:1–3.

5 Judges 16.

him, Israel more broadly) into idolatry.[6] Before him, David ran into his own problems. Known as a man after God's own heart,[7] he fell into grievous sin when he was not where he was supposed to be—leading his army in battle.[8] Instead, he stayed behind and was distracted by lust for Bathsheba, leading him into a spiral of sin that ultimately resulted in adultery and the orchestrated murder of Bathsheba's husband. Even the mightiest men, when distracted or disengaged from their mission, can be led astray by lesser things.

The minor sins Screwtape champions, along with the endless distractions that divert our eye from being single to God's glory, lull us into a false sense of security. Men today are in danger of falling into this trap, allowing lesser things to consume their time and energy while they neglect the weightier matters of their mission. We are induced into spiritual sleep by the very culture that surrounds us—one that pacifies with convenience, entertainment, and idolatrous obsessions. Before we realize it, our time and energy have been drained, flaxen cords fastened, and our stewardship becomes squandered. To rise up, men must first see lesser things for what they are—tools of subtle enslavement designed to keep them from their true mission. Let's review a few.

The Praise of Men

While translating the Book of Mormon, Joseph Smith was approached by Martin Harris, a wealthy and influential man

6 1 Kings 11:1–6.
7 1 Samuel 13:14.
8 2 Samuel 11:1.

who had financially supported the translation project. Harris, eager to prove the legitimacy of the work to his skeptical wife and associates, repeatedly asked Joseph to let him take the manuscript of the first 116 pages—two months' worth of work—to show to others. Despite being warned by the Lord not to let the pages leave his possession, Joseph, under increasing pressure from Harris, sought the Lord's permission several times. Eventually, the Lord relented and allowed Joseph to lend the manuscript, but only under strict conditions.

Joseph's decision to appease Harris was a choice rooted in a fear of man over fear of God. The outcome was seemingly disastrous—the 116 pages were lost, and with them, a key portion of the Book of Mormon's record. Joseph was understandably heartbroken, and the work of translation was halted for a time as a consequence.[9] Through this experience, Joseph learned the vital lesson that the praise of men—even from those with influence and authority—should never take precedence over God's will. This lesson came in the form of a divine rebuke:

> For although a man may have many revelations, and have power to do many mighty works, yet if he boasts in his own strength, and sets at naught the counsels of God, and follows after the dictates of his own will and carnal desires, he must fall and incur the vengeance of a just God upon him. Behold, you have been entrusted with these things, but how strict were your commandments; and remember also the promises which were made to you, if you did not transgress them.

9 D&C 10:1–2.

> And behold, how oft you have transgressed the commandments and the laws of God, and have gone on in the persuasions of men. For, behold, you should not have feared man more than God. Although men set at naught the counsels of God, and despise his words—yet you should have been faithful; and he would have extended his arm and supported you against all the fiery darts of the adversary; and he would have been with you in every time of trouble.[10]

When we fear what others will think or proactively seek their praise, we elevate the opinions and priorities of our fallible peers over those of our infallible Father. Jesus rightly rebuked the Pharisees who "loved the praise of men more than the praise of God."[11] They're not an exception to the rule, of course; people generally, and God's people specifically, have repeatedly fallen from grace by chasing after the approval of those around them. Nephi warned of latter-day movements that would likewise be "built up to become popular in the eyes of the world,"[12] having previously echoed Isaiah's words cautioning us: "Fear ye not the reproach of men, neither be ye afraid of their revilings."[13]

Of course, we know from Lehi's vision what happens to those who prioritize the praise of peers over the commands of God; those who heeded the scorn and sought the approval of the multitude in the great and spacious building wandered

10 D&C 3:4–8.
11 John 12:43.
12 1 Nephi 22:23.
13 2 Nephi 8:7.

away and became lost.[14] We read these scriptures, we know them well—and yet it's often difficult to actually apply their lessons. In a practical sense, it's quite tempting to want praise from others. The natural man—indeed, our very brains—condition us to seek it. The external stimuli from praise ignite a neurochemical party in our brain, with dopamine, serotonin, and oxytocin producing a physical reaction that makes us feel good. We implicitly seek more of this good feeling, our brain rewarding us for the behaviors that produce this response. But like any party, too much of a good thing can become bad. Pretty soon, people spend hours doomscrolling on social media, reshaping their personality to be as appealing to others as possible, losing themselves in the process. This desire for validation can lead men to compromise their values and adopt behaviors that are contrary to their spiritual goals. Instead of being grounded in their relationship with God, they are driven by the ever-shifting opinions of others. As Lehi's vision illustrates, the pursuit of worldly praise is hollow and fleeting, ultimately leading to spiritual disorientation and destruction.

No wonder the Savior warned, "Woe unto you when all men shall speak well of you!"[15] Christ understood that seeking the praise of men often means diluting our discipleship. Following God requires loyalty to His will, regardless of how it is perceived by the world. Those who chase after the approval of others may find temporary satisfaction, but they lose the eternal rewards that come from standing firm in their convictions. Just as the Nephites and Joseph Smith experienced,

---

14 1 Nephi 8.
15 Luke 6:26.

the praise of men is a fleeting and unreliable foundation upon which to build one's life. The temptation to seek it can often feel innocent, even noble, as we desire acceptance or validation for our efforts. But as Christ taught of those who want the glory of men, "they have their reward"[16]—one that pales in comparison to the eternal blessings that come from seeking first the kingdom of God. The challenge for each of us is to resist the lure of worldly accolades and to remain steadfast in our devotion to God's higher purposes. Let's contrast and compare what this might look like:

Lesser Thing	Greater Thing
Embracing what is popular	Embracing what is right
Seeking validation through social media	Seeking approval from God through righteous living
Pursuing worldly success for recognition	Pursuing personal growth for eternal progress
Acting out of fear of rejection	Acting out of faith in God's plan
Prioritizing external appearances	Prioritizing inner spiritual strength

16 Matthew 6:2.

Lesser Thing	Greater Thing
Modifying beliefs to fit societal trends	Standing firm in gospel principles
Compromising values to please others	Holding fast to integrity, regardless of opinion
Measuring worth by others' opinions	Measuring worth by your divine identity
Following the crowd for acceptance	Leading by example in righteousness

Ultimately, pursuing the praise of men is a shallow and fleeting endeavor, one that distracts us from our true purpose and binds us with the very flaxen cords we are warned against. It leads us to compromise, to seek validation in superficial ways, and to abandon the deeper, eternal truths that define our divine identity. To rise up, we must reject the temptation to conform to worldly standards and instead focus on what truly matters: pleasing God, promoting truth, and doing what is right regardless of social trends and peer pressure. Men of conviction are guided by the will of the Almighty rather than the whims of society.[17]

Mammon

One of Christ's would-be disciples once asked him, "What shall I do that I may inherit eternal life?" Jesus responded by

17 D&C 121:34–38.

reminding him of the commandments he already knew: do not commit adultery, kill, steal, or bear false witness, and honor your parents. The young man acknowledged these prerequisites and replied that "All these have I observed from my youth." And then Jesus pinpointed his problem: "One thing thou lackest: go thy way, sell whatsoever thou hast, and give to the poor, and thou shalt have treasure in heaven: and come, take up the cross, and follow me."[18] Sadly, the young man was grieved by this expectation and consequently failed the test, "for he had great possessions."[19]

This is a particular challenge for modern men in a capitalist society who are told and expected to be providers. We're supposed to build and sustain, generating an income to support ourselves and others. But we must also remember that money is merely a means to an end—not an end in itself. What matters more is the purpose for which it's acquired and how it's used. Money is not the root of all evil, according to the apostle Paul—the *love* of money is.[20] Our love—our attention and loyalty—can only be focused in a single direction at a time. "No man can serve two masters," Jesus explained, "for either he will hate the one, and love the other; or else he will hold to the one, and despise the other."[21] To the degree that we give our affection to idols and false gods, we withhold it from our God. And Jesus had a particular idol in mind, for in

18 Mark 10:17–21.
19 Mark 10:22.
20 1 Timothy 6:10.
21 Matthew 6:24.

the next sentence he concluded, "Ye cannot serve God and mammon."

The word mammon comes from an Aramaic word meaning wealth. It can be interpreted as an idol of materialism, one that entices people to "worship the work of their own hands, that which their own fingers have made."[22] Seduced by the benefits that wealth brings, many pursue the "vain things of this world"—power, property, and prominence. Alma taught that "you cannot carry [these things] with you,"[23] just as Jesus explained that those who lay up for themselves "treasures upon earth" demonstrate by their actions where their heart (and its love) truly is.[24] Men constantly fail this test, prompting Moroni to lament, "Why do ye adorn yourselves with that which hath no life...?"[25]

In a stern address to his family and friends, Nephi's brother Jacob pointed out how early riches had already led many of them to become "lifted up in the pride of your hearts,"[26] persecuting those they perceived to be less fortunate. He admonished them to be "free with your substance, that they may be rich like unto you"[27]—repeating a call for charity that Christ and His prophets have repeatedly shared through scripture. He continued:

> But before ye seek for riches, seek ye for the kingdom of God. And after ye have obtained a hope in Christ ye

22 2 Nephi 12:8.
23 Alma 39:14.
24 Matthew 6:19–21.
25 Mormon 8:39.
26 Jacob 2:13.
27 Jacob 2:17.

> shall obtain riches, if ye seek them; and ye will seek them for the intent to do good—to clothe the naked, and to feed the hungry, and to liberate the captive, and administer relief to the sick and the afflicted.[28]

As Hugh Nibley once wrote, "Every step in the direction of increasing one's personal holdings is a step away from Zion."[29] God gives to the giver; the resources of this earth are meant to be shared with all, for "there is enough, and to spare."[30] Yes, we men are and ought to be providers—but we must remember to prioritize God and recognize our wealth as a stewardship rather than an ownership. We are custodians for these resources that exist to help support our families and others' families as well. The most important thing is to keep the most important thing the most important thing. In a culture obsessed with mammon and its perceived benefits of power, property, and prominence, we must avoid lesser things and keep God and His purposes the most important thing. Here's the contrast:

Lesser Thing	Greater Thing
Pursuing wealth for personal gain	Pursuing wealth to do good and serve others

28 Jacob 2:18–19.

29 Hugh Nibley, *Approaching Zion* (Salt Lake City: Deseret Book Company, 1989), 37.

30 D&C 104:15–17; immediately prior to this the Lord discusses how He wishes to provide for His saints, by exalting the poor and making the rich low.

Lesser Thing	Greater Thing
Prioritizing material possessions	Prioritizing the kingdom of God
Loving money and what it can buy	Loving God and His purposes
Measuring success by worldly wealth	Measuring success by spiritual progress
Building personal wealth	Building up Zion
Hoarding resources	Sharing generously
Seeing oneself as an owner	Seeing oneself as a steward
Chasing temporary treasures on earth	Storing up treasures in heaven

Money is a tool—a means of achieving a particular end. In that sense, it tests our ability to faithfully manage the resources God places in our hands for wise stewardship. Whether we pass the test or not hinges on how we use the money we acquire. Do we hoard it for personal gain or do we deploy it in the service of God and His children? Wealth is fleeting, but the impact we make with it, the lives we uplift, and the causes we champion for good endure beyond the grave. Ultimately, our purpose is not to amass treasures on earth but to store treasures in heaven by using our resources compassionately, generously, and wisely. If we can master mammon, we will prove ourselves worthy stewards in God's eternal economy—blessed not for what we possess, but for how we have used what was entrusted to us to build His kingdom. Will we be men of mammon, like nearly everyone around us, or men of God, prioritizing His purposes?

The Arm of Flesh

Fifty-six years after the Declaration of Independence was signed, a community of Latter-day Saints in Missouri was viciously attacked by a mob of their disgruntled neighbors. Having lost their homes, their loved ones, and their possessions, those who survived understandably felt a desire for retaliation and revenge. After all, this latest bout of persecution was not a unique occurrence. Time and again, these people had been subjected to similar oppression. Some surely wanted revenge.

In the midst of such intense feelings and contentious circumstances, the Lord gave a revelation in response. Despite the people's strong desire to strike back, God instructed them to "renounce war and proclaim peace."[31] They were instructed to "first lift a standard of peace,"[32] to bear attacks patiently, "and revile not against [the aggressor], neither seek revenge"[33]—a clear rebuke of a culture that condones and encourages retaliatory strikes against one's enemies. In fact, only after three offenses (or acts of aggression) committed against us, each of which we should meet with forgiveness,

31 D&C 98:16.
32 D&C 98:34.
33 D&C 98:23.

does the Lord tell us that "thine enemy is in thine hands and thou art justified" in "going out to battle against that nation."[34]

This is a tough pill to swallow for men who see themselves as protectors. We've been raised on stories of Captain Moroni raising the Title of Liberty or the stripling warriors rising up against their enemies. Yet in this modern revelation, the Lord made clear that this higher standard—forgiving one's enemies, bearing attacks patiently, and seeking God's protection and support—applies to everyone, as "an ensample unto all people, saith the Lord your God, for justification before me."[35]

Scriptural history is full of examples where God's people rejected His protection in favor of trying to provide their own. But we also see numerous evidences where they did avoid relying on the "arm of flesh" to instead rely on the Lord. For example, when the King of Assyria attacked Judah, his invading army was much bigger than that of the Jews. But King Hezekiah noted that "with him is an arm of flesh, but with us is the Lord our God to help us, and to fight our battles."[36] David echoed similar words when going against Goliath.[37] When the Syrians surrounded Israel with their large host, Elisha's servant was predictably worried. "Alas, my master! how shall we do?" he fretted. Elisha responded: "Fear not: for they that be with us are more than they that be with them."[38] These stories remind us of God's protection for righteous people who seek

34 D&C 98:31, 36.
35 D&C 98:38.
36 2 Chronicles 32:8.
37 1 Samuel 17:45.
38 2 Kings 6:14-17.

His strength over our own—who rely on His arm instead of the arm of flesh. "We should not fear our enemies," Mormon explains, but rather "fear [our] God and... supplicate him for protection."[39]

We're not doing great in this regard today, and haven't been for decades. Clear back in 1976, President Spencer W. Kimball rebuked Christ's disciples for relying on the arm of flesh as an idol:

> In spite of our delight in defining ourselves as modern, and our tendency to think we possess a sophistication that no people in the past ever had—in spite of these things, we are, on the whole, an idolatrous people—a condition most repugnant to the Lord.
>
> We are a warlike people, easily distracted from our assignment of preparing for the coming of the Lord. When enemies rise up, we commit vast resources to the fabrication of gods of stone and steel—ships, planes, missiles, fortifications—and depend on them for protection and deliverance. When threatened, we become antienemy instead of pro-kingdom of God; we train a man in the art of war and call him a patriot, thus, in the manner of Satan's counterfeit of true patriotism, perverting the Savior's teaching:
>
> "Love your enemies, bless them that curse you, do good to them that hate you, and pray for them which despitefully use you, and persecute you; That ye may

---

39 3 Nephi 4:10.

> be the children of your Father which is in heaven" (Matt. 5:44–45).
>
> We forget that if we are righteous the Lord will either not suffer our enemies to come upon us... or he will fight our battles for us...[40]

Rising up from these lesser things demands that we proactively renounce war and forgive our enemies—a truly countercultural stance, especially in times when the drums of war beat ever louder. As then-Elder Dallin H. Oaks once said, peace "is not just the absence of war; it is the *opposite* of war."[41] We must be peace*makers*—something very difficult to accomplish in an environment of militaristic idolatry and counterfeit patriotism. The arm of flesh is perhaps the most seductive of idols because it is so widely justified and embraced. The "gods of stone and steel" receive our adoration and support, and we often view ourselves as dependent on them, while God is rendered comparatively powerless. We begin to worship God as a distant being who helps us when we lose our car keys or when a loved one has cancer, but who does not intervene in physical conflict when lives are on the line. Christians thus relegate the Savior to the spiritual realm only, viewing Him as unable to protect them in the way soldiers and military arsenals clearly can. The counterfeit thus

---

40 Spencer W. Kimball, "The False Gods We Worship," *Ensign*, June 1976, https://www.churchofjesuschrist.org/study/ensign/1976/06/the-false-gods-we-worship.

41 Dallin H. Oaks, "World Peace," *Ensign*, May 1990, https://www.churchofjesuschrist.org/study/general-conference/1990/04/world-peace.

becomes the accepted norm, leading God's people to abandon Him in favor of fleshy idols. Christ is relegated to the back seat in terms of the average believer's consideration of their physical safety, if He is even invited into the vehicle at all.

What would it look like to abandon our idolatry and rely more on God?

Lesser Thing	Greater Thing
Relying on the arm of flesh	Relying on the arm of God
Trusting in weapons of war for safety	Trusting in God's power to defend and protect
Worshiping "gods of stone and steel"	Worshiping God as the source of all deliverance
Seeking retaliation or revenge	Renouncing war and pro-claiming peace
Embracing counterfeit patriotism	Loving and forgiving our enemies
Fearing physical enemies	Fearing God
Elevating military power over spiritual power	Elevating spiritual strength as the ultimate defense
Viewing Christ as distant and uninvolved	Trusting Christ as the ultimate protector

God has commanded men not to be protectors but peacemakers. Peacemaking is not the byproduct of soldiers, drones, and munitions. It instead comes from living the gospel of Jesus Christ. It requires loving our enemies,[42] forgiving those who have wronged us,[43] raising a standard of peace to those who actually attack us,[44] and in all things renouncing war and proclaiming peace.[45] True discipleship demands that we reject the counterfeit security offered by the arm of flesh and instead place our trust in the Savior, whose teachings challenge the world's notions of power and protection. The path of peace is not passive or weak; it is bold, countercultural, and deeply transformative, aligning us with divine power rather than mortal might. By choosing peace, we rise above the lesser things of this world and become true instruments in the hands of God, participating in His higher work of redemption and reconciliation.

Carnal Desires

The Nephite society had a lot of promise. The Lord and His prophets repeatedly assured the Nephites of great blessings if they remained faithful and obedient. For instance, Lehi promised his descendants that they would prosper in the land as long as they kept the commandments of God.[46] King Benjamin highlighted the prosperity and protection that would

---

42 Matthew 5:44.
43 Matthew 18:21, D&C 98:40.
44 D&C 98:34.
45 D&C 98:16.
46 2 Nephi 1:20.

come to those who followed the Lord's path.[47] Time and again, the Nephites were reminded that they were a chosen people, and that great blessings—both temporal and spiritual—were theirs for the taking, contingent on their righteousness.

And then they snatched defeat from the jaws of victory. What did them in? Was it the frequent attacks by Lamanite armies? Not at all; external conflict frequently resulted in *more* righteousness, as Nephites supplicated themselves to God for protection in trying times.[48] The Nephite society didn't wither under the pressure of external forces—it imploded due to internal degradation. They repeatedly struggled with pride, inequality, and forgetting God. And when conflict arose, many dissenters defected to the Lamanites, stoking their anger against the Nephites and inciting them to launch an attack. In one case, they succeeded in prodding the Lamanites to obtain "all the possession of the Nephites which was in the land southward."[49] Moronihah and the Nephite army had limited success in later regaining some of their lands, but they had suffered many losses. Here's how Mormon explains their circumstance:

> Now this great loss of the Nephites, and the great slaughter which was among them, would not have happened had it not been for their wickedness and their abomination which was among them; yea, and it was among those also who professed to belong to the church of God.

---

47 Mosiah 2:22.
48 2 Nephi 5:25; Mosiah 9:16–17; Alma 2:27–28; Alma 43:49–50; Alma 58:10–12. See Helaman 4:23–25 for the opposite.
49 Helaman 4:8.

> And it was because of the pride of their hearts, because of their exceeding riches, yea, it was because of their oppression to the poor, withholding their food from the hungry, withholding their clothing from the naked, and smiting their humble brethren upon the cheek, making a mock of that which was sacred, denying the spirit of prophecy and of revelation, murdering, plundering, lying, stealing, committing adultery, rising up in great contentions, and deserting away into the land of Nephi, among the Lamanites—
>
> And because of this their great wickedness, and their boastings in their own strength, they were left in their own strength; therefore they did not prosper, but were afflicted and smitten, and driven before the Lamanites, until they had lost possession of almost all their lands.[50]

In the space of seven short years after this, secret combinations had amassed significant power and wealth. The now-righteous Lamanites repelled these hostile forces and preached the word of God to them,[51] whereas the corrupted Nephites "did build them up and support them, beginning at the more wicked part of them, until they had overspread all the land of the Nephites, and had seduced the more part of the righteous until they had come down to believe in their works and partake of their spoils, and to join with them in their secret murders and combinations."[52] As they became increas-

50 Helaman 4:11–13.
51 Helaman 6:37.
52 Helaman 6:38.

ingly indulgent in worldly pleasures, the Nephites' hearts hardened and their moral compass faltered. The promise of wealth and power appealed to their baser instincts, drawing them away from righteousness. Instead of shunning evil, they began to rationalize their actions, no doubt blinded by the desire for immediate gratification. In their quest for material gain and social dominance, they willingly participated in the corruption that eroded their society from within. What began as small concessions to carnal desires soon led them down a path of spiritual decay, until even the righteous were seduced into the web of deceit and violence.

While we're taught to keep our eye single to God's glory,[53] we are easily distracted by the abundance of seductive distractions that tempt us. Certainly, the lure of power and wealth pulls us away from God and toward mammon, as do a number of other carnal desires that besiege modern men. Top of the list might be pornography, which well over two-thirds of men regularly view.[54] Its addictive nature is well-documented, with studies showing that it rewires the brain, creating pathways that crave constant stimulation and novelty.[55] What begins as curiosity or a momentary lapse of discipline quickly escalates into a compulsive habit, consuming a man's thoughts and energy. It distorts his view of relationships and

---

53 D&C 4:5; 88:67–68.

54 R. Ballester-Arnal, M. García-Barba, J. Castro-Calvo, et al., "Pornography Consumption in People of Different Age Groups: an Analysis Based on Gender, Contents, and Consequences," *Sexuality Research and Social Policy*, 766–779 (2023).

55 Todd Love, et al. "Neuroscience of Internet Pornography Addiction: A Review and Update," *Behavioral Sciences* (Basel, Switzerland) vol. 5,3 388-433. 18 Sep. 2015.

intimacy, reducing others to mere objects of desire and hollowing out the depth and meaning of genuine connection. This addiction not only isolates a man from his loved ones but also builds a barrier between him and God, making it difficult for him to feel the Spirit and hear divine promptings. Cravings that are temporarily satisfying keep us bound to a cycle of consumption and self-indulgence. Over time, they become habits that numb our spiritual sensitivities, making it harder to hear God's voice and easier to justify further indulgence.

Of course, there are countless other carnal desires that could qualify as lesser things. Overindulgence in sports, entertainment, and recreational activities can consume countless hours, pulling attention away from more meaningful pursuits. Social media, with its endless distractions and dopamine-driven doomscrolling, reduces our ability to be present and focused, let alone create space for introspection, prayer, or meaningful interaction with loved ones. Similarly, gluttony and a lack of physical self-discipline can diminish our overall well-being, leading to neglect of the body and mind that God has given us to use for higher purposes. Consuming intoxicating or harmful substances—yes, including energy or sugary drinks—can cloud our judgment and destroy our ability to exercise self-control. Even idleness or laziness, where we neglect responsibilities in favor of regular leisure, keeps us from fulfilling our duties to family, community, and God. Each of these desires may appear harmless at first, but can easily become destructive patterns that draw us further away from the path God wants us to follow. The contrast could not be more clear:

Lesser Thing	Greater Thing
Overindulging in sports and entertainment	Prioritizing time for spiritual growth and service
Chasing dopamine through social media and distractions	Seeking deeper connections with God and loved ones
Numbing with gluttony and lack of self-discipline	Practicing moderation and treating the body as a temple
Consuming intoxicating or addictive substances	Keeping a clear mind to be open to spiritual guidance
Neglecting responsibilities in favor of leisure	Embracing work, service, and duty as paths to fulfillment
Consuming pornography and focusing on short-term pleasures	Developing genuine intimacy and avoiding things that can harm our long-term goals
Pursuing physical pleasure above all else	Seeking lasting joy through spiritual connection
Living in constant distraction and busyness	Finding stillness to hear God's voice and feel the Spirit

The carnal desires that consume our attention and turn our hearts away from God are not unlike the lures that enticed the Nephites to support secret combinations and forsake Him. These desires may seem insignificant at first, some less dangerous or sinful than others, but they gradually erode our spiritual strength and make us vulnerable to greater evils. At scale, they cause society to decay. If we are to avoid the fate of the Nephites, we must recognize these distractions for what they are and rise up to reclaim our focus on what truly matters.

Caesar

Jesus was born into a world of sociopolitical tension. Many Jews believed themselves to be living in the last days and yearned for the long-promised Messiah to save them from their oppressive rulers and become their new political king. As the disciples of Jesus began applying the label to Him, it was not a simple platitude—there was a very real hope that Christ would be a sort of warrior priest, assembling an army to overthrow both the Herodian dynasty and the Roman occupation. Israel's story, frankly, is one of occupation—including Egypt, Assyria, Babylon, Persia, and Greece at different times. Each empire claimed political authority over the children of Israel, supplanting God's laws with their own. Calling Jesus their Messiah meant that Christ's followers saw him as the Anointed One, the foretold king who would save God's people and rule over them in righteousness.

When bloodthirsty Jews later pushed back on Pilate and demanded Christ's murder, he asked the group, "Shall I crucify your King?" The chief priests remarkably replied: "We have no king but Caesar."[56] In one simple statement, the spiritually empty religious establishment sided with the state and against God. And ever since then, those who claim to worship God have instead served the various Caesars of their day, counterfeit gods each of them, whether in the form of Pharaoh or President, Führer or King. Like the one true God, these substitutions demand loyalty, assert their divine authority, desire our worship, and offer protection from the enemy.[57] But behind all of these cheap fakes is Lucifer, who sees earthly possessions as his. He is so brazen that even to Christ he said: "All this power will I give thee, and the glory of them: for that is delivered unto me; and to whomsoever I will I give it. If thou therefore wilt worship me, all shall be thine."[58] Jesus rightly refused his hollow promises and claim to power that mankind repeatedly accepts. Adam's son Cain was the first to fall prey to Satan's promise that one can "murder and get gain,"[59] and then get away with it. Countless others throughout world history—especially those in positions of political power—have similarly "entered into a covenant with Satan, after the manner of Cain."[60]

---

56 John 19:15.

57 For a breakdown of each characteristic see Connor Boyack, *Christ versus Caesar: Two Masters, One Choice* (Springville: Cedar Fort, 2020), 17–20.

58 Luke 4:5–7.

59 Moses 5:31.

60 Moses 5:49. See also Ether 8:22–23 and 11:15.

Most Christians have not themselves entered into this covenant, of course, nor do they see their submission to government as involvement in a Satanic plot. But their participation in Caesar's processes and partaking of his spoils make them complicit—like their spiritual forebears, attempting to serve two masters at once,[61] thus qualifying themselves to instead be rejected by God.[62] By placing their trust in earthly rulers and turning to them as a source of prosperity and protection, they contribute to a system that mimics true divine authority, yet ultimately serves a different master. This misplaced trust in political powers, as a source of security and salvation, draws believers away from the need to rely on God's guidance and protection. Just as the chief priests' declaration revealed a deeper allegiance to the worldly power of Rome over the divine authority of Christ, many Christians today inadvertently make similar choices when they prioritize political "solutions" over spiritual ones.

God wants men to be anxiously engaged in good causes—to "do many things of their own free will, and bring to pass much righteousness" as independent agents.[63] We don't delegate our agency to bureaucratic middlemen, outsourcing our responsibilities to the government. When commanded to help the poor, we do so directly rather than tolerating an inefficient welfare system that relies on coercively taken tax revenue. When commanded to teach our children, we rise up to fulfill this parental obligation and opportunity rather than

61 Matthew 6:24.
62 Revelation 3:15–16; Matthew 25:11–12.
63 D&C 58:27–28.

relying on Caesar's indoctrination centers. When commanded to forgive our enemies and lift up a standard of peace to those who attack us, we don't turn to Caesar's gods of stone and steel to be our source of deliverance and strength. And when commanded to abstain from intoxicating substances and carnal abominations such as pornography, we fight these influences with persuasion instead of using Caesar's tools to ban them and forcibly punish those who partake.

This is certainly not any easy path, given how interwoven into our culture Caesar has long been; since the beginning of man, Lucifer has been promising power and offering the earth's riches to those who cooperate with him. But disciples of Christ are called to choose Him, and that requires a clear separation from the status quo that looks like this:

Lesser Thing	Greater Thing
Trusting in government for security	Trusting in God's protection
Relying on political power to create change	Relying on the transformative power of the gospel
Bowing to the demands of the state	Following Christ's commandments
Viewing political leaders as saviors	Recognizing Jesus Christ as the only true Savior

Lesser Thing	Greater Thing
Pursuing worldly power and influence	Pursuing spiritual growth and humility
Fighting enemies through force	Loving and forgiving enemies
Prioritizing allegiance to the nation	Prioritizing allegiance to God and His kingdom
Finding identity in citizenship of a country	Finding identity as a disciple of Christ

Choosing Christ over Caesar comes with its own challenges and sacrifices. But as followers of Christ, we are called to rise above the seductive comforts of worldly power and walk a different path—a path that may seem narrow and difficult but ultimately leads to greater peace and freedom. To avoid the fate of the foolish Israelites who declared their loyalty to Caesar, we must remember that no earthly power is a valid substitute for God's and that true discipleship means rejecting all counterfeits that would draw our hearts away from Him.

—∾—

The pitfalls of prioritizing lesser things are clearly evident throughout the scriptures for those who have the eyes to see. All of God's children—and particularly the men who bear His priesthood—are called to a higher purpose, yet they often settle for distractions, indulgences, and misplaced loyalties that keep them from rising to their full potential. Whether it's the allure of wealth, the praise of men, the promise of power, or the comforts of entertainment, each of these diversions weakens our spiritual strength and draws us away from God's path. The adversary is content to see us ensnared in these traps, knowing that they bind us as effectively as more overt acts of rebellion.

These lesser things often operate on our minds like the adversary himself does, convincing us of their irrelevance or nonexistence so that we can contentedly convince ourselves that all is well in our lives individually, and Zion collectively.[64] Over and over, God's people delude themselves into thinking they're sufficiently righteous while embracing all kinds of idolatry and sin. Jesus excoriated the Pharisees who would nitpick details of one's superficial worship while omitting "the weightier matters of the law"—calling them "blind guides, which strain at a gnat, and swallow a camel."[65] The Zoramites basked in their self-deception, deluding themselves into thinking they were "a chosen and a holy people" while wholeheartedly embracing what Alma called "the vain things of the world."[66] In Revelation, we read of one group of God's people whose prosperity led them into spiritual apathy, feeling that they had "need of nothing," while being unaware that God considered them to be "wretched, and miserable, and poor, and blind, and naked."[67]

64 2 Nephi 28:21.
65 Matthew 23:23–28.
66 Alma 31:18, 27.
67 Revelation 3:17.

This is not a new trend—in fact, it's one of the oldest. Yet people continue down these well-worn paths, led by blind guides. In both ancient and modern times, God has observed that "all flesh had corrupted his way upon the earth,"[68] where "none doeth good, for all have gone out of the way."[69] These errant fools—including plenty, and perhaps most, of so-called "active Church members"—are those of whom the Lord spoke:

> They seek not the Lord to establish his righteousness, but every man walketh in his own way, and after the image of his own god, whose image is in the likeness of the world, and whose substance is that of an idol, which waxeth old and shall perish in Babylon, even Babylon the great, which shall fall.[70]

Our task is to buck the trend and avoid this fate that has befallen so many of our spiritual peers. Instead of assuming that these clear scriptural patterns don't apply to us, we should frankly consider ourselves the guilty party about whom past prophets have warned.[71] Rather than thinking ourselves righteous while others are spiritually inferior, we should recognize that the Lord's condemnations apply just as much—indeed, much *more*—to us than they do to those who have not received such spiritual privilege.

On the final night of his mortal ministry, Jesus broke bread with His disciples and ominously revealed, "One of you shall betray me." It would be natural to be defensive in such a situ-

68 Genesis 6:12.
69 D&C 82:6.
70 D&C 1:16.
71 Mormon 8:28–41; 2 Nephi 27:1–5; Isaiah 28:7–8.

ation. *Surely Jesus is talking about someone else—not me!* But nobody pointed fingers or asked Him if the guilty party was a particular person they suspected. Instead, "they were exceeding sorrowful, and began every one of them to say unto him, Lord, is it I?"[72] Their questions were personal; they were applying the Savior's prophecy to themselves. We should learn from their example.

Too many men today are mired in spiritual mediocrity. They—we—are distracted, and our path deviated by lesser things that increase our distance from God. Such men chase after wealth, entertainment, status, or worldly pleasures, believing that these pursuits will bring fulfillment. Or if they haven't consciously sought after such things, they have passively pursued them as a result of social conditioning and the "traditions of our fathers."[73] They casually follow the crowd and its Babylonian practices, embracing idolatry while convincing themselves they are still on the covenant path.

This self-deception allows men to rationalize their indulgence in lesser things while neglecting their divine potential. Rather than rising up as warriors for truth and righteousness, they are lulled into spiritual sleep, content with superficial worship and worldly pursuits. Remember that the adversary's greatest tool isn't always blatant sin—distraction and diversion are typically better at eroding faith and compromising God's children.

If we are to be men of God, we must consciously and courageously cast aside these lesser things—identifying and avoid-

72 Matthew 26:21–22.
73 Enos 1:14.

ing them to realign our hearts with eternal priorities. Only then will we rise above the mediocrity that entraps many and become the men God needs us to be—men of faith, integrity, and purpose, sharing the light of the gospel in a world increasingly consumed by darkness.

HEART AND SOUL

I am a graduate of what I like to call the public fool system. Growing up in San Diego, California, in the 1980s, it was what everyone did; the government schools were where all kids were sent, and few parents (except the supposedly weird ones) questioned it. And like hundreds of millions of kids before me, I was subjected to government-approved propaganda without realizing it. I accepted what I was taught by authority figures, who had the position to dictate my academic fate. I complied without question because that's what everyone else was doing (and because I was just a kid).

This commentary applies as much to the curriculum itself as it does to something like the Pledge of Allegiance. There I stood, day after day, hand over my heart, mindlessly reciting words I had been trained to memorize as an impressionable child. It was ritualistic, mechanical, and devoid of substance. It was as if I were a soldier at morning roll call responding robotically to orders given. I didn't even understand what I was saying.

I felt this same way years later when I was living in the Missionary Training Center, learning how to teach the gospel to investigators—and in another language to boot. Every morning, our class would stand and recite from the Doctrine and Covenants: "Now behold, a marvelous work is about to come forth among the children of men. Therefore, O ye that embark in the service of God, see that ye serve him with all your heart, might, mind and strength, that ye may stand blameless before God at the last day.[1]" While I certainly had a deeper connection to these words than I did as a child to the Pledge of Allegiance, I realize in retrospect that there was a similar ritualistic, mechanical approach to the daily recitation—and that there wasn't much substance. I still didn't understand what I was saying.

God doesn't want part of our allegiance, nor does he want it pledged robotically. He doesn't want summertime soldiers in the battle for truth, half-heartedly marching to orders they don't fully comprehend. He despises when we're lukewarm,[2] choosing between two masters[3] without fully committing to Him. God wants disciples who are fully engaged—in particular, men who internalize His teachings and live by them with conviction. Serving God with all our heart, might, mind, and strength must be more than a memorized phrase; it's a call to action, a complete surrender of self to the cause of righteousness.

But how often do we, like my younger self, go through the motions of spiritual commitment without fully engaging? How often do we recite scriptures, attend meetings, or even perform service while our hearts and minds are somewhere else, distracted by lesser things? It's easy to become passive participants, doing just enough to check the boxes without

1 D&C 4:1–2.
2 Revelation 3:16.
3 Matthew 6:24.

truly offering our all—contenting ourselves, because of our outward motions, to feel sufficiently righteous and obedient. Yet, the Lord's expectation is clear: He wants every part of us—our deepest desires, our mental focus, our physical energy, and our spiritual strength—all aligned with His will and purpose. Like C.S. Lewis once wrote, "Christ says, 'Give me All. I don't want so much of your time and so much of your money and so much of your work: I want You.'"[4]

Imagine what that might look like for you—rising up above the lesser things in life and committing your all to God. What would your prayers look like—your conversation with your Father—if you brought your whole soul to the interaction and developed a next-level intimacy? How much wealthier would you be if the resources God had blessed you with as a steward were consecrated to further His work and bless His children? How much spiritual power would you possess if you treated repentance seriously and developed a deeper sensitivity to any deviation from God? What hidden truths and mysteries would be revealed if your gospel study moved from milk to meat with profound curiosity? Imagine rising up so high above the world's lesser things that God sees fit to send an angel to instruct you. Consider how powerful an instrument in His hands you could become—how pleased He would be with you for your commitment to His will.

God's constant displeasure is recorded throughout scripture—a chronicle of disappointment with His children apostatizing again and again. This includes those, like the foolish

---

4 C.S. Lewis, *Mere Christianity* (New York: HarperCollins, 1996), 196.

virgins or Church-going masses, whose hearts remain far from Him and who are insincere Saints serving another master. But their fate is not yours, nor is it written anywhere that this outcome is universal or inevitable. There are always exceptions to the rule. And where the rule is idolatry and apostasy, you can be the exception. You *must* be the exception.

In a world so often filled with spiritual mediocrity and complacency, God is calling for men who will rise above—the few who will be chosen[5]—who will not settle for the status quo. He needs men who will stand as beacons of light in a world drowning in darkness, whose lives are testimonies of dedication, purity, and faith. The Lord does not expect perfection, but He does demand effort, intention, and sincerity. The question is not whether you will struggle—because you will—but whether you will fight those struggles with everything you have: your heart, soul, mind, and strength.

Heart

Nebuchadnezzar was a narcissist. Like other kings before him, he thought a lot of himself and loved the benefits his power and position afforded him. Reflecting a cultural landscape steeped in idolatry and absolute power, the Babylonian monarch erected a massive golden statue—90 feet tall and 9 feet wide—in a central location meant for his subjects to worship. We do not know if the image was of himself (plausible, given how kings would deify themselves to reinforce their au-

5 D&C 121:34.

thority) or of a Babylonian deity such as Marduk.[6] What we do know is its purpose: this statue symbolized absolute power and demanded unwavering loyalty from his subjects. Nebuchadnezzar commanded his subjects to bow down to the image whenever they heard the sound of music, a ritual meant to reinforce both obedience and conformity across the kingdom. Those who failed to worship would be "cast into the midst of a burning fiery furnace."[7]

The Bible says, in its typical exaggerated language, that "all the people, the nations, and the languages, fell down and worshipped the golden image that Nebuchadnezzar the king had set up."[8] This is not true, of course; not everyone complied. Among other likely acts of civil disobedience not recorded, we read of Shadrach, Meshach, and Abed-nego—three Jewish men of rank in the Babylonian government—who opted out and boldly told the king, "We will not serve thy gods, nor worship the golden image which thou hast set up."[9] Furious at their disobedience, Nebuchadnezzar had them thrown into the fire, where God protected them, surprising the king and prompting him to promote them.[10]

We might not always be so fortunate, but the commandment is clear: "Thou shalt have no other gods before me."[11] It was the first commandment given through Moses to the rescued children of Israel, who were subsequently told not

---

6 Marduk rose from being a minor agricultural deity to the chief god of Babylon and eventually the head of the Mesopotamian pantheon. His prominence bordered on monotheism, as he absorbed attributes of other gods and acquired 50 divine names signifying his supremacy.

7 Daniel 3:6.

8 Daniel 3:7.

9 Daniel 3:18.

10 Daniel 3:26–30.

11 Exodus 20:3.

to bow down or serve these other Gods.[12] Having lived for generations in Egypt—a society steeped in polytheism and idolatry—God's chosen people had been surrounded and influenced by a culture that worshiped numerous gods, each with specific forms, powers, and purposes. After centuries in such an environment, the Israelites had become culturally conditioned to a way of life where idolatry was normalized. When God delivered them from bondage, He was not only rescuing them physically but also spiritually, calling them to a new way of life centered on exclusive devotion to Him.

This is perhaps best summarized by God's explanation that he is a "jealous God,"[13] one who is offended when our affections and loyalties are diverted to any degree from Him. In any close relationship—as in a marriage or between ourselves and God—we ought to give our heart to the other person. This is a deep, emotional commitment, grounded in vulnerability, that signifies we're all-in. In a spiritual context, this means avoiding at all costs the actions of so many of God's children who were seduced by surrounding cultural beliefs and practices, creating a syncretic religion—one that was rooted in the gospel but intertwined with idolatry. We can't claim to be happily married while having a "side chick"; no man can serve two masters.[14]

What idolatry entices us today? Surely we are more enlightened than the ancient Israelites who "walked in the statutes of the heathen" and "feared other gods," going so far as

12 Exodus 20:5.
13 Ibid.
14 Matthew 6:24.

to build altars to these gods right in their communities in order to more easily participate in pagan rituals.[15] Right? We are faithfully monotheistic, for starters; most of us would not be caught dead worshiping a golden calf or anything like it. While physical idols may not attract as many adherents, spiritual ones certainly do. They're more sophisticated and modern than their tangible predecessors. They're easier to hide and thus harder for others to detect. It's easier to segment our heart and split our loyalty when the act is not as overt as a public display of idolatrous adoration. Our idolatry is a function of the portion of our heart we allow to be seduced away by the lesser things that pull us down from God's presence. Let's briefly review each of them and consider how giving our heart to God helps us rise up above the lesser things in our lives.

The Praise of Men. We know that "man looketh on the outward appearance, but the Lord looketh on the heart."[16] The natural man is a superficial creature, one who is stimulated by social approval and the praise of peers. Overcoming these tendencies requires us to recognize their influence and our biological predisposition to them. To give our heart fully to God, we must shift our focus from external validation to internal conviction. The praise of men is shallow and fleeting, a moving target that requires us to constantly adjust, compromise, and mask our true selves to fit the mold of public opin-

15 2 Kings 17:7–13.
16 1 Samuel 16:7.

ion. But when we give our heart to God, we place our worth in something unchanging and eternal.

Mammon. Christ taught plainly that "Ye cannot serve God and mammon,"[17] underscoring the dichotomy between building up God's kingdom versus attempting to build up our own. Mammon represents both money and a mindset that places material gain, comfort, and security above spiritual priorities. The temptation to serve mammon is seductive because it appeals to our desire for stability, status, and self-sufficiency. But giving our heart to God means that we must view money as a tool, not a master, and a means to serve rather than a reason to serve. We are to see ourselves as stewards of God's treasures, as opposed to owners of our own. When our hearts are seduced by the spoils of this world, we become tempted to sacrifice principles for profit. But by choosing God over mammon, we free ourselves from the empty promises of materialism and embrace a life where true fulfillment comes from a relationship with the Creator, not the accumulation of man-made creations.

The Arm of Flesh. Trusting in the arm of flesh represents our tendency to rely on human strength, wisdom, or resources rather than placing full confidence in God. Throughout scripture, God warns His people not to depend on man-made systems or human power for security and salvation. All too often, we fail. When the COVID-19 pandemic broke out, for exam-

17 Matthew 6:24.

ple, Christ's followers for the most part placed their hope in pharmaceutical solutions instead of relying on the Lord and heeding His counsel. Instead of seeking revelation for what could stave off the virus and using priesthood power to bring healing to the afflicted, Church leaders praised a rushed, untested vaccine as a "literal godsend"[18] that was "proven to be both safe and effective"[19]—a completely untrue claim. (No such proof existed, and, as it turned out, the vaccines were neither safe nor effective.) They "urge[d] individuals to be vaccinated"[20] and pushed social distancing and face masking, none of which were medically necessary or helpful. When we rely on worldly strength, we tether ourselves to something fallible and ultimately limited. Giving our heart to God requires acknowledging that He alone is our protector and provider. Like anyone we give our heart to, we trust Him—especially in times of peril. Instead, the Saints too often buy into secular propaganda and look to the arm of flesh to save them from perceived threats. In future circumstances, we must rise up above the urge to rely on worldly solutions that distract from divine guidance.

---

18 "President Russell M. Nelson and the COVID-19 vaccine: What the church leader has said and done," *Deseret News*, April 29, 2021, https://www.deseret.com/faith/2021/4/29/22407953/president-nelson-on-covid-19-vaccine-comments-speeches-actions-prayers-shot-church-news/.

19 "Church's First Presidency urges vaccination, says vaccines are 'safe and effective' in battle with COVID-19," *Deseret News*, August 12, 2021, https://www.deseret.com/faith/2021/8/12/22621678/latter-day-saints-lds-church-mormon-leaders-support-covid-vaccine-masks/.

20 Ibid.

Carnal Desires. The Nephites snatched defeat from the jaws of victory by corrupting their righteous, prosperous society as they pursued prideful, vain pleasures. They failed to guard their hearts and honor their loyalty to God—and thus became a spiritually idolatrous people like so many of God's children before them. This is a common downfall for anyone enticed by physical gratification over lasting spiritual fulfillment. Modern temptations—whether pornography, endless entertainment, or even social media distractions—work similarly, capturing our attention and binding us to cycles of carnal consumption. These desires, often indulged in small ways, can consume more of our thoughts, energy, and focus than we realize, dulling our spiritual senses and distancing us from God. Giving our heart to God requires intentional resistance to these temptations and a readiness to rise above momentary pleasures. By doing so, we nurture a deeper relationship with God centered on spiritual purpose rather than temporal indulgence.

Caesar. Giving our heart to God means keeping our loyalty and allegiance fixed on Him. We must steer clear of worldly substitutes and idolatrous stand-ins who desire the same level of loyalty. Throughout history, people have looked to earthly powers for security, prosperity, and solutions, often at the cost of their spiritual fidelity. When we place our trust in government, look to political leaders for salvation, or rely on human systems for deliverance, we are committing spiritual adultery against a jealous God. Christ's example is clear: despite the allure of political power and earthly rule,

He refused to bow to Satan's offers and chose the path of persuasion and service instead. As modern-day disciples, we are called to make the same choice, pursuing change through voluntary and persuasive means, not the coercive arm of Caesar that compels others to fall in line. Trusting God over Caesar means rejecting the false promises of human institutions and embracing the higher law of love, forgiveness, and direct responsibility in fulfilling God's commandments. In doing so, we recognize Christ as our only King and commit fully to His divine authority, even when the comforts of worldly power would tempt us otherwise.

Let's also be careful to realize that giving our heart to God is not the whole deal; serving and loving God inevitably implies doing the same for His children[21]—our family, our neighbors, our colleagues, and even those who may ridicule or mistreat us. Giving our heart to God means trust and commitment, so we need to bring that same effort to our interpersonal relationships in the here and now. "Inasmuch as ye do it unto the least of these," the Lord said, "ye do it unto me."[22] This means we must mourn with those who mourn, minister to others not based on assignments but on organic and sincere relationships, go after the one, and forgive all who have done us wrong just as we would forgive our closest loved ones.

In a world full of distractions that pull us away from the path to God, we must repeatedly remember—in a literal, proactive sense—the heavenly treasures that are our only real

21 Matthew 25:37–40.
22 D&C 42:38.

goal in life. Others pursue ephemeral pleasures and have their reward;[23] our eyes must remain on the eternal prize. "For where your treasure is, there will your heart be also," the Savior taught.[24] If we want to rise up above the lesser things, we need to guard our hearts from the seductive idols that want our loyalty and affection. Many before us have failed. We must not.

Soul

Alma the Younger was a consummate rebel—a "very wicked and an idolatrous man"[25]— as were his accomplices, the sons of Mosiah. Together, they divided the church community and led many astray in an attempt to "destroy the church of God."[26] After an angelic visitation and an accelerated conversion to the gospel, Alma shared the observation that "My soul was racked with eternal torment; but I am snatched, and my soul is pained no more."[27] The ensuing missionary work from this former band of religious renegades was centered around the soul. These men "were desirous that salvation should be declared to every creature, for they could not bear that any human soul should perish; yea, even the very thoughts that any soul should endure endless torment did cause them to quake and tremble."[28]

---

23 Matthew 6:2.
24 Matthew 6:21.
25 Mosiah 27:8.
26 Mosiah 27:10.
27 Mosiah 27:29.
28 Mosiah 28:3.

The scriptures are full of references to one's soul. Jesus commanded us to "love the Lord thy God… with all thy soul."[29] In the modern dispensation, He reminded us that "the worth of souls is great in the sight of God."[30] Our soul can be cheated by Satan[31] and enlarged by the Lord.[32] The sacrament is blessed and sanctified to the souls who partake of it[33] so that our "soul shall never hunger nor thirst, but shall be filled."[34] But what exactly *is* a soul? It's one of those words we often read but rarely clarify. We are not necessarily aided by Webster's 1828 Dictionary—a go-to resource for understanding terms found in restoration-era scripture. Webster lists fifteen different definitions! In his view, the soul can be a "spirit," or "the intellectual principle," or "a human being."[35] Here's how one Church manual defines it:

> In scripture, the term soul is used as a synonym for spirit to describe a person in four different phases of his or her eternal existence. Soul is used to describe a person in premortal life—before birth. During earth life, the soul is joined with a physical body. At death, the soul leaves the body and goes to the spirit world to await resurrection. In the Resurrection, the body and

---

29 Matthew 23:37.
30 D&C 18:10.
31 2 Nephi 28:21.
32 Alma 32:28.
33 D&C 20:77–79.
34 3 Nephi 20:8.
35 "Soul," American Dictionary of the English Language, accessed November 29, 2024, https://webstersdictionary1828.com/Dictionary/soul.

> soul are inseparably connected, which is called "the redemption of the soul."[36]

So Webster was on track, especially with the definitions calling the soul "an intelligent being" or "immortal substance in man."[37] Loving God is, therefore, a combined physical and spiritual act—using our entire person to worship Him. That means aligning both our beliefs and our actions, without any inconsistency between what we claim to believe and what our choices reveal about us. This isn't a theology that tolerates half-measures, with only *part* of one's soul regarded as enough to dedicate to God. Instead, we are to "offer your whole souls as an offering unto him."[38] The phrase "whole soul" (or its plural form) appears in the Book of Mormon seven times,[39] the added emphasis making clear that this is an all-or-nothing endeavor.

God commands us to dedicate our *whole* souls to Him because He is willing to do the same for us. In the Old Testament, God states, "I will rejoice over them to do them good, and I will plant them in this land assuredly with my whole heart and with my whole soul."[40] This divine reciprocity underscores the depth of God's love and commitment to each of us—to *you*. When He asks for our whole soul, it is not a demand from a divine dictator but an invitation to enter into

---

36 "Soul," Gospel Topics, The Church of Jesus Christ of Latter-day Saints, https://www.churchofjesuschrist.org/study/manual/gospel-topics/soul?lang=eng.

37 "Soul," American Dictionary of the English Language.

38 Omni 1:26.

39 See 2 Nephi 25:29; Enos 1:9; Omni 1:26; Words of Mormon 1:18; Mosiah 2:20–21; 26:14; Alma 11:37.

40 Jeremiah 32:41.

a covenant relationship where both parties are fully invested. Giving us Jesus Christ was the ultimate demonstration of this commitment, offering salvation to all who would accept Him. Christ's atonement exemplifies what it means to dedicate one's whole soul—He gave everything, holding nothing back, to fulfill the Father's will and secure our eternal happiness.

The principle of offering your whole soul is inherently forward-looking. It challenges us to consider the eternal consequences of our choices, urging us to prioritize what will bring lasting joy and fulfillment over fleeting pleasure. Our "future selves"—glorified beings capable of inheriting all that God has—become the vision that can inspire us to be done with lesser things and rise up above spiritual death. Simply avoiding sin and enduring to the end isn't enough; we must proactively demonstrate our commitment to Christ through every facet of our lives—with our whole soul. This is how we begin to fulfill God's charge to "care for the soul, and for the life of the soul"[41]—something that Elder Maxwell rightly pointed out is our task "on any day, in any decade, amid any decadence and destruction."[42]

Easier said than done, right? Life is full of distractions and temptations that compete for our attention, inviting us to reserve space in our soul for them. Many are benign, some are destructive; either way, these obstacles keep us down spiritu-

41 D&C 101:37.

42 Neal A. Maxwell, "Care for the Life of the Soul," *Ensign*, May 2003, https://www.churchofjesuschrist.org/study/general-conference/2003/04/care-for-the-life-of-the-soul?lang=eng.

ally. How do we rise up? Let's review how dedicating our soul to God can help us overcome the lesser things in our lives.

The Praise of Men. Christ rebuked the Pharisees who loved "the praise of men more than the praise of God."[43] In this, we are all Pharisees—each of us neurobiologically wired to crave the dopamine hit that flattery provides. Like junk food for the body, the praise of men offers a fleeting rush that satisfies for a moment but ultimately leaves our souls malnourished and dependent on more. Scriptural stories abound of people being led astray by manipulative individuals who exploited this carnal craving, using flattery to praise others in order to gain power over them. In contrast, our soul thrives on the nourishing sustenance of eternal truths—the kind that strengthens and sustains us for the long haul, amid decadence and destruction and everything in-between. To give our soul fully to God, we must break free from the lure of superficial validation and seek the spiritual nourishment found in His love and approval. The more we detach from the empty calories of worldly adulation, the more we fortify our soul, enabling it to rise above the noise and embrace the lasting joy of God's infinite approval—the only one that actually matters.

Mammon. Our soul was made for spiritual purposes, but is seduced by worldly ones. It won't thrive when divided between eternal priorities and material pursuits. The pull of materialism is strong, enticing us with promises of security, status, and

43 John 12:43.

satisfaction. Yet these promises are fleeting, and their pursuit often leaves the soul empty and disconnected from its divine source. Christ's counsel to "lay up for yourselves treasures in heaven"[44] reminds us that our soul's eternal reward requires rising up above mammon. This means prioritizing generosity over greed, stewardship over ownership, and trusting in God's provision rather than in the fleeting guarantees of material wealth. We do not own what we possess; we are merely caretakers of God's resources to use for our families and to bless the lives of others. Mammon is more than money—it's a mindset that places worldly gain and comfort above spiritual devotion. It is corrosive to our souls.

The Arm of Flesh. When we seek security for our soul through human strength and political maneuvering, we fracture our fidelity to God and forfeit the divine help that only He can provide. Consider Gideon's army, whittled down from thousands to a mere three hundred men—armed not with swords and chariots, but with trumpets and torches—to highlight that victory is the Lord's to give.[45] This unexpected triumph offers a warning to readers who have eyes to see, that the arm of flesh, no matter how well-trained or well-equipped, will always fail us in comparison to God's infinite power. Giving our whole soul to God means resisting the temptation to resolve conflicts through coercion and control—rather, we surrender control to our King. It means exchanging the false security of gods of stone and steel for the deliverance God has promised

44 Matthew 6:19–21.
45 Judges 7.

the faithful. This is perhaps particularly hard for men to do, who see it as one of their roles to be protectors of their family. But by rejecting the counterfeit comforts of the weak arm of flesh, we can instead rely on the Lord's powerful arm.

Carnal Desires. Nephite society after Christ's visit to the Americas was nearly heaven on earth—a new Zion where "there were no contentions and disputations among them, and every man did deal justly one with another."[46] More than merely being nice, "they had all things common among them"[47]—an astounding economic evolution from the pride cycle that had previously plagued their community. Yet even such profound spiritual prosperity could crumble, and indeed, it eventually did, due primarily to yielding once more to carnal desires.[48] Overcoming these temptations requires more than occasional self-restraint—it demands a total surrender of our soul's focus from temporary pleasures to eternal rewards. This choice involves consistent spiritual practices like meaningful prayer, fasting, and studying God's word, all designed to recalibrate our desires and realign our souls with His will. Joseph's example in fleeing Potiphar's wife underscores that resisting carnal desires is less about suppressing temptation and more about preserving our relationship with God.[49] Practically, it involves consciously curating our daily influences—friendships, entertainment, and environments—to ensure

46 4 Nephi 1:2.
47 4 Nephi 1:3.
48 4 Nephi 1:24, 28, 34.
49 Genesis 39:7–12.

they strengthen rather than undermine our spiritual resolve. By giving our entire soul to God, we find that carnal impulses lose their grip, replaced by an abiding hunger for righteousness and divine companionship, empowering us to rise above lesser things and secure the enduring joy of true discipleship.

Caesar. During an infamous 1973 bank robbery in Stockholm, Sweden, hostages formed emotional bonds with their captors, even defending them after their release.[50] This phenomenon, now known as Stockholm Syndrome, describes how victims, driven by a distorted sense of survival, begin sympathizing with and even supporting their aggressors. Spiritually, we face a similar condition with Caesar—earthly governments and political authorities. Caesar, at its core, is a bully, employing institutionalized violence and coercion that directly oppose Christ's teachings of love, compassion, and voluntary action. Yet, tragically, many professed followers of Christ proudly pledge their allegiance to national identities and political powers, willingly sacrificing significant parts of their souls to institutions built on force rather than faith. Giving our soul fully to Christ means clearly and consciously rejecting loyalty to Caesar. We must anchor our identity and allegiance exclusively in God's kingdom, resisting mortal counterfeits that promise security but deliver spiritual bondage. Building Zion requires actions motivated by genuine persuasion and love, steadfastly refusing Caesar's tempting offer to compel

50 Christopher Klein, "Stockholm Syndrome: The True Story of Hostages Loyal to Their Captor," History.com, April 9, 2019, https://www.history.com/news/stockholm-syndrome.

righteousness. Only when our souls are devoted entirely to Christ, rather than earthly governments, can we experience the true freedom, peace, and integrity that God desires for us.

Pouring out our whole soul to God as men means embracing total honesty, complete engagement, and unwavering commitment—qualities often challenging to cultivate amid competing pressures and distractions of a busy life. It's not always (or ever?) easy to engage in extended prayer and reflection like Enos and Mormon did.[51] In addition, we men frequently grapple with pride, independence, and self-sufficiency, mistakenly viewing vulnerability and spiritual dependence as weaknesses rather than strengths. Our struggle lies in acknowledging our reliance on God and surrendering control, recognizing that true strength comes from our relationship with and connection to our Heavenly Father.

Dedicating our whole soul to God involves intentionally aligning our priorities with His. It requires consistently honoring our covenants, not just during Sunday worship, but throughout all aspects of our daily lives. To genuinely rise above lesser things, we must reject compartmentalizing our faith into a separate "religious bucket" reserved solely for Sundays and occasional acts of service. Instead, we allow our faith to permeate every dimension of our lives—our whole soul—by applying Christ's teachings to all our interactions, be they political, economic, familial, or otherwise. We believe in and act upon God's word, as consistently as possible, each and

51 Enos 1:4; Mormon 3:12.

every day—relying on repentance when we veer off course. By devoting our souls to God, we gain the courage to lead and become the men of integrity and spiritual strength that God calls us to be.

Mind

Once Neo woke up in *The Matrix*, he was extremely confused. The world he thought was real turned out to be fiction. He couldn't comprehend what was happening, so Morpheus took him into a training program where he explained:

> The Matrix is a system, Neo. That system is our enemy. But when you're inside, you look around, what do you see? Businessmen, teachers, lawyers, carpenters. The very minds of the people we are trying to save. But until we do, these people are still a part of that system and that makes them our enemy. You have to understand, most of these people are not ready to be unplugged. And many of them are so inured, so hopelessly dependent on the system, that they will fight to protect it.

Just moments before, Neo was hopelessly dependent on that same system. But by taking the red pill, he woke up to reality after emerging from a carefully constructed fantasy designed to influence his every decision. Though unsettling at first, Neo was now experiencing "things as they really are"—the foundation of truth.[52] This reality empowered him

---

52 Jacob 4:13.

to think clearly and act decisively. He could act, rather than only being acted upon.[53]

Truth, by its very nature, is liberating. As Jesus said, once you know the truth, "the truth shall make you free."[54] Being informed with truth equips us to recognize deception and better exercise our agency. Moroni explained that understanding truth is what allows us to "know good from evil."[55] If we are confused about objective reality and God's truths, then we are disoriented and disempowered, unable to effectively act as His agents. But when we seek, embrace, and internalize truth, we are empowered to align our decisions with God's eternal purposes, freeing ourselves from manipulation by false doctrines, cultural pressures, and misleading worldly narratives. Only through a clear comprehension of truth can we truly become masters of our choices, proactively moving God's work forward rather than passively succumbing to adversarial influences.

Imagine a despot ruling over a nation. Does this tyrant want a citizenry composed of informed individuals? Or does he prefer them to be ignorant? The question answers itself, of course. Those who seek power over us—and the devil by whom they are influenced—prefer we be intellectually subdued. After all, if we are unfamiliar with the problems of the past, we'll be less likely to solve them in the present and future. (Tangentially, this is why governments operate education systems, in order to control historical narratives and bury

53 2 Nephi 2:14, 16, 26.
54 John 8:32.
55 Moroni 7:15.

unflattering information that might challenge their past actions and present claim to authority.) Hence why the scriptures, in particular the Book of Mormon (over 180 times![56]), repeatedly challenge us to *remember* the past—"not only to *say*, but to *do*" what God commanded of us.[57]

Like Neo, each of us is called to embrace truth—and to do that we must wake up from the spiritual slumber of a manufactured reality. Isaiah calls upon us to "Awake, awake, put on strength."[58] Lehi challenged his rebellious sons to "awake from a deep sleep... and shake off the awful chains by which ye are bound."[59] Paul said, "Awake, thou that sleepest, and arise from the dead."[60] Moroni challenged us to "awake to a sense of [our] awful situation."[61] And in one of the final verses of the compiled record, he tells us to "awake, and arise from the dust."[62] When these and other prophets urged their people and their own children to awake, they did so recognizing that many were spiritually asleep, drifting through life oblivious to the deeper truths and realities around them. They were caught up in false narratives and limited vision, subtly shaped by falsehoods designed to limit their freedom and separate them from God.

56 "'To Stir Them Up in the Ways of Remembrance': Lamanites and Memory in the Book of Mormon," *Religious Educator*, vol. 6, no. 3, 2005, https://rsc.byu.edu/vol-6-no-3-2005/stir-them-ways-remembrance-lamanites-memory-book-mormon.

57 D&C 84:57; emphasis added.

58 Isaiah 51:9.

59 2 Nephi 1:13.

60 Ephesians 5:14

61 Ether 8:24.

62 Moroni 10:31.

To overcome lesser things, we must give our mind to God by cultivating intellectual awareness and discernment. We need to understand the patterns and mistakes of the past to avoid repeating them. We need "knowledge of things as they are, and as they were, and as they are to come."[63] God was pretty comprehensive in outlining the things we ought to study and know:

> Teach ye diligently and my grace shall attend you, that you may be instructed more perfectly in theory, in principle, in doctrine, in the law of the gospel, in all things that pertain unto the kingdom of God, that are expedient for you to understand;
>
> Of things both in heaven and in the earth, and under the earth; things which have been, things which are, things which must shortly come to pass; things which are at home, things which are abroad; the wars and the perplexities of the nations, and the judgments which are on the land; and a knowledge also of countries and of kingdoms—
>
> That ye may be prepared in all things when I shall send you again to magnify the calling whereunto I have called you, and the mission with which I have commissioned you.[64]

Giving our minds to God does not mean passively accepting teachings from counterfeit authorities or merely believing

63 D&C 93:24.
64 D&C 88:78–80.

what we are told. To the contrary—the more we learn, the more we realize how many falsehoods and deceptions exist that were blinding us and continue to blind others.[65] Instead, we actively use our God-given minds to seek and discern truth, distinguishing between divine insights and disguised deceptions. Overcoming the lesser things that pull us down and keep us in deep slumber demands that we become awake, alert, and informed, empowering us to become "an instrument in his hands in bringing so many of [our peers] to a knowledge of his truth."[66] Let's review how giving our mind to serve the King of Kings can help us rise up above the lesser things in our lives.

The Praise of Men. Our brains are wired to crave approval, activating reward pathways similar to those involved in addictive behaviors. Extensive research demonstrates how social acceptance activates reward systems in the brain and influences our behavior. As one neuroscientist wrote, "The self is more of a superhighway for social influence than it is the impenetrable private fortress we believe it to be."[67] We are easily conditioned by those around us—particularly when we are young and crave peer acceptance. Understanding this limitation allows us to mitigate its downsides; as the famed G.I. Joe cartoon taught, "Knowing is half the battle." By using our mind to navigate the brain's limitations, we can recognize

---

65 D&C 123:12.

66 Mosiah 23:10.

67 Matthew D. Lieberman, *Social: Why Our Brains Are Wired to Connect* (New York: Crown Publishers, 2013), 4.

the hollowness of worldly validation and the manipulative intent often behind flattery. Instead, we can deliberately redirect our thoughts toward seeking eternal truths and divine approval rather than fleeting human praise. This intentional mental shift empowers us to detach from superficial affirmations, grounding our identity firmly in Christ and freeing our minds from the subtle traps designed to distract and compromise us.

Mammon. Giving our mind to God empowers us to discern the true value of things, helping us overcome mammon's enticing illusions. An intellect that understands God's revealed truths recognizes the fleeting nature of material wealth and the emptiness that follows excessive pursuit of possessions. We are smart enough to see through and resist the pervasive manipulations of consumer culture that continually urge us toward dissatisfaction, debt, and endless acquisition. When our thoughts align with eternal principles, we clearly understand our role as stewards—not owners—of earthly resources, promoting gratitude rather than greed. By intentionally focusing our thoughts on spiritual realities rather than temporal illusions, we achieve genuine freedom from mammon's grasp and confidently invest in treasures of lasting worth.

The Arm of Flesh. King Mosiah provides a powerful example of overcoming the arm of flesh by thoughtfully using his mental faculties. After studying the Jaredite record,[68] Mosiah

68 Mosiah 28:17.

recognized a recurring and destructive pattern—monarchical governments inevitably succumbed to corruption, violence, and oppression.[69] This rational understanding allowed him to act decisively, dismantling the monarchy over which he himself reigned and establishing a decentralized system, encouraging his people to rely on self-governance rooted in divine law rather than the flawed strength of human authority.[70] Mosiah resisted the manipulative allure of centralized power—despite himself being its apex—knowing it often breeds dependence on flawed human rulers rather than reliance on the Lord.[71] His intellectual discernment empowered him to reject political strategies that exploit fear and offer false assurances, demonstrating to his people—and to us—that the surest protection from the pitfalls of the arm of flesh lies in aligning our minds (and actions!) with God's eternal truths.

Carnal Desires. Samson's tragic downfall illustrates what happens when our minds are disconnected from God and governed instead by unchecked carnal desires. Despite immense physical strength, Samson's intellectual blindness to the dangers of immediate gratification and his failure to reflect on the lasting consequences of his choices left him vulnerable to Delilah's deception.[72] By contrast, when we consciously dedicate our minds to God, we become equipped to recognize the seductive illusion of instant pleasure and understand its de-

69 Mosiah 29:7.
70 Mosiah 29:5.
71 Mosiah 29:17.
72 Judges 13–16.

structive long-term outcomes. This spiritual and intellectual awareness enables us to mindfully identify and resist temptations, redirecting our focus toward lasting fulfillment rather than fleeting gratification.

Caesar. When we dedicate our minds to God, we seek out and learn from the lessons of history, observing patterns of corruption and abuse inherent in the rule of mortal men. Historical awareness reveals a consistent reality: governments have repeatedly been instruments wielded by the adversary to centralize power, enrich rulers, and exploit those they govern. Understanding this allows us to see through the empty promises and alluring rhetoric of modern politicians who seek our loyalty by glorifying the state and whitewashing its misdeeds. With a mind attuned to divine truths and informed by historical evidence, we become less susceptible to manipulation, discerning the hidden motives behind appeals to patriotism and nationalism. This intellectual clarity empowers us to reserve our ultimate allegiance for Christ alone, guarding us against being ensnared by counterfeit authorities that seek to bind our minds and souls under their dominion.

To fully give our minds to God, we must challenge our assumptions and question beliefs we've long held without scrutiny. No tradition of our fathers should be shielded from this review. The process requires courage—not merely intellectual assent—to investigate uncomfortable truths that may unsettle our complacency or threaten our cherished traditions. A committed mind isn't content with the superficiality of inherited knowledge; rather, it eagerly pursues deeper understanding, actively seeks hidden wisdom, and persistently questions narratives shaped by worldly interests. Doing so isn't simply an intellectual exercise—it's an act of worship and devotion, demonstrating genuine humility before God and sincere readiness to be taught by Him. We show our willingness to use the mental power He provided and expects us to use.

Ultimately, a mind dedicated to God is one actively shaped by His truths rather than passively molded by worldly influences. This alignment grants us a clarity of vision that not only helps us identify deceptions but empowers us to constructively help others, leading them out of spiritual darkness toward the greater understanding we've received. As our minds become clearer, our discernment sharper, and our convictions deeper, we become increasingly effective instruments in God's hands—capable of influencing our families, communities, and even societies for good. Giving our minds fully to God thus becomes not just personal protection against deception but a powerful means of spreading truth, elevating others, and building His kingdom on earth.

Strength

In the fall of 2024, while on a trip in Germany, I visited Plötzensee Prison, which opened all the way back in 1879. Today, it houses common criminals, a third of whom are incarcerated for repeated public transport fare evasion.[73] But

73 "Strafen: Jeder Dritte in Plötzensee sitzt wegen Schwarzfahrens," Tagesspiegel, December 15, 2008, https://www.tagesspiegel.de/berlin/jeder-dritte-in-plotzensee-sitzt-wegen-

a memorial center adjacent to the prison chronicles a time when its residents were largely political prisoners. Plötzensee during the Nazi era was one of the main sites for administering capital punishment—state-sanctioned murder.

My travel companions wandered through one of the memorial's rooms, in which various photos and stories are shared of some of the roughly 3,000 inmates who were executed during this period. But I fixated on the next room over, connected only by a small metal door through which the inmate would be taken to be put to death. This room had a concrete floor and plastered white walls and stood empty, with a few arrangements of flowers placed near the two small windows at the far end. The only other feature of note—and one upon which my gaze was transfixed—was a drain in the center of the room. Above this drain, decades ago, stood a guillotine to sever the inmates' heads; the drain allowed the flow of blood to not pool in the heavily used room. It was on this precise spot where I stood—hallowed ground, in my estimation—where, among the thousands that Nazi officials murdered, the youngest person executed by the German state courageously met his death on a crisp October evening in 1942.

Helmuth Hübener was no stranger to opposition, nor did he shirk from it. In his earlier teen years, a Hitler Youth patrol stopped him and his friends on the street after overhearing them sing American songs. "Why shouldn't we sing them?" Helmuth rebuked them. "It's not against the law!"[74] The in-

---

schwarzfahrens-8598460.html.

74 Rudi Wobbe and Jerry Borrowman, *Before the Blood Tribunal* (American Fork: Covenant Communications, 1992), 21.

quisitors left, but Helmuth was still upset. "That's the trouble with these people—put them in a uniform and they think they have the authority to bully people around," he told his friends. "It doesn't matter whether they belong to the Hitler Youth, the SA, or the SS... Our country is being run through threats, intimidation, and even brutal force! And something has to be done about this!"[75]

Another incident influenced Helmuth and his conspiring friends, all members of the Church. At the age of sixty-six, Heinrich Worbs, one of the small branch's most devout members, was arrested by the Gestapo and sent to a concentration camp for six months. Someone had overheard him comment, after seeing a Nazi monument, "Another statute for one of those Nazi butchers!" and reported him.[76] When Worbs later returned to his congregation, he was a shell of his former self after having been severely tortured during his imprisonment. Six weeks later, he died. "What upset Helmuth and me the most," one of Helmuth's friends, Rudi Wobbe, said, "was the way the other members of our congregation treated Brother Worbs upon his return. Rather than rally to his defense to comfort him, many turned a cold shoulder, refusing to speak to him. He was ostracized because he 'kicked against the pricks' by opposing the government."[77]

Despite the "Extraordinary Radio Measures" decree by Nazi Propaganda Minister Joseph Goebbels, which made listening to foreign radio stations a crime punishable by im-

---

75 Ibid.
76 Ibid., 25–26.
77 Ibid., 26.

prisonment—with distribution of information gleaned from foreign broadcasts qualifying for the death penalty—Helmuth secretly listened to his half-brother's radio to hear war reports from the BBC. Seeing the ridiculously embellished German propaganda for what it was, Helmuth used a Church typewriter to begin producing leaflets to educate and warn his countrymen. "Down with Hitler," read one of the first he produced. More followed, each of them taking aim at German propaganda. He also took direct aim at party officials. The Führer "will send you by the thousands into the fires in order to finish the crime he started," Helmuth wrote in one leaflet. "By the thousands your wives and children will become widows and orphans. And for nothing!"[78]

Over the course of ten months, Helmuth produced twenty-nine leaflets, each of them barbed and provocative—and with the help of his accomplices, distributed more than one thousand copies in mailboxes, telephone booths, bulletin boards, coat pockets, and more. Compelled by his faith, he chose to stand up while others who professed his same faith remained silently seated—or, in the case of his branch president, fought and rebuked his efforts. Helmuth hoped to spark a revolution and dethrone Hitler. Instead, he met the guillotine.

Whether Helmuth's courageous defiance was wise, given the overwhelming Nazi regime he opposed, can be debated, yet his intentional and focused effort toward a righteous cause cannot. This is precisely what God asks when He calls upon

78 Helmuth Hübener, "I've Calculated for Everything," Document 42 in Holmes and Keele, eds. and trans., When Truth Was Treason, 208.

us to serve Him with all our strength.[79] Our strength is the combination of exerting our physical and mental energy in pursuit of a stated goal. God commanded that "men should be anxiously engaged in a good cause, and do many things of their own free will, and bring to pass much righteousness."[80] He wants us to apply our effort to effecting positive change—and reveals in the next verse that "the power is in [us]."[81] That power is potential energy, like gasoline in your vehicle or water held behind a dam. Only when you turn your car key to begin igniting the gasoline, or when the dam opens to allow water through, is the energy released and applied toward an outcome. We, too, must act in order to use the power that is in us to bring to pass much righteousness. Our potential energy is only meaningful when converted into purposeful action.

We are charged to "be not weary in well-doing"[82] and to actively "waste and wear out our lives in bringing to light all the hidden things of darkness."[83] We cannot fulfill these commandments when we are bound by the "awful chains"[84] forged from the consequences of our poor choices, which alienate us from God. Perhaps this is one very small silver lining in the dark cloud of war in which Helmuth lived—such intense adversity tends to strip away distractions and indulgences that easily captivate our attention in times of comfort and abundance. When confronted by profound moral clarity and ex-

79 D&C 4:1–2.
80 D&C 58:27.
81 D&C 58:28.
82 D&C 64:33.
83 D&C 123:13.
84 2 Nephi 1:13.

istential threats, trivial concerns lose their allure, helping us sharpen our focus on what truly matters. Yet, we don't need to wait for an authoritarian state or extreme circumstances to awaken us to what matters most. We can proactively dedicate our strength to building God's kingdom even during times of peace and normalcy. Let's explore how using our strength in the service of God empowers us to rise above lesser things.

The Praise of Men. Giving our strength to God means actively channeling our energy into endeavors that please Him rather than those that attract worldly admiration. Consider Captain Moroni, who tirelessly fortified his people both physically and spiritually, working diligently "not for power, but to pull it down" and "not for honor of the world, but for the glory of [our] God."[85] Moroni devoted his strength to a righteous cause without seeking personal acclaim or recognition. Similarly, John the Baptist declared, in reference to his cousin Jesus, "He must increase, but I must decrease,"[86] willingly exerting his strength—even unto death—to magnify Christ rather than himself. When our energies are committed to God's purposes rather than the superficial allure of human approval, we become capable of rising above the hollow praise of men. Our labor then contributes meaningfully to the establishment of God's kingdom, bringing lasting joy and satisfaction beyond any temporary applause the world could ever offer.

---

85 Alma 60:36.
86 John 3:30.

Mammon. We reap what we sow—and if we use our strength to sow things that build God's kingdom, we are more likely to avoid building our own by pursuing "treasures upon earth, where moth and rust doth corrupt."[87] The early Saints in Acts, like the Nephites after Christ's visit, exemplify this principle; they devoted their energy to spiritual pursuits, shared their resources generously, and lived with "all things common,"[88] effectively overcoming mammon's powerful pull. Similarly, King Benjamin tirelessly served his people, declaring that he had labored with his own hands to prevent burdening them with taxes or tribute, demonstrating that his strength was directed toward selfless service rather than self-enrichment.[89] When we actively invest our physical energy and resources into service, generosity, and spiritual endeavors, we reinforce our freedom from mammon's grasp, empowering ourselves to pursue eternal treasures that bring fulfillment and lasting peace.

The Arm of Flesh. Many today fall into the same spiritual lethargy that once plagued ancient Israel, preferring to delegate their responsibilities to earthly authorities rather than exerting personal effort in service to God. When the Israelites demanded a king to rule them "like all the nations,"[90] they effectively sought relief from the rigorous demands of direct reliance upon and active participation with the Lord. Similarly, in our time, the temptation is strong to rely on

87 Matthew 6:19.
88 Acts 2:44–45; 4 Nephi 1:3.
89 Mosiah 2:14.
90 1 Samuel 8:5.

governments, institutions, or charismatic leaders, allowing them to shoulder tasks we find burdensome or inconvenient. But scripture repeatedly warns of the consequences awaiting slothful servants.[91] Shirking our spiritual duties weakens our personal growth and undermines our divine potential. Instead, we must actively choose personal engagement over passive dependence, thereby becoming empowered instruments in God's hands.

Carnal Desires. "Idle hands are the devil's workshop," goes the familiar proverb—a reminder that inactivity can easily lead to spiritual vulnerability. When we fail to actively channel our energy into meaningful, righteous endeavors, we become susceptible to the alluring distractions of carnal desires. King David's tragic fall with Bathsheba exemplifies this danger; instead of actively leading his troops on the battlefield, David remained idle at home, providing opportunity for temptation to overtake him.[92] Conversely, those who proactively dedicate their strength to God's service find little time or energy for destructive pursuits. By intentionally focusing our efforts on praiseworthy pursuits, we displace opportunities for temptation. Rust doesn't form on a frequently used blade.

Caesar. When we actively dedicate our strength to God, we prioritize personal responsibility to care for ourselves, our families, and our communities voluntarily. This effort reduces our dependence on Caesar's institutions, freeing us from the

---

91 Matthew 25:14–30; D&C 58:26–29, 107:100.
92 2 Samuel 11:1–4.

spiritual and temporal chains that come with reliance upon state power. Caesar claims our strength through coercion—taxation, war, and enforced compliance—demanding our energy and resources for purposes often in direct opposition to Christ's teachings. By contrast, Christ invites us to voluntarily commit our strength to service, charity, and sacrifice, fostering peace and genuine compassion. Using our physical and spiritual energy to build God's kingdom empowers us to reject Caesar's deceptive offers of security and control, enabling us instead to build Christ-centered communities rooted in voluntary cooperation, self-reliance, and neighborly love.

We were created to be agents who act rather than passive beings who are merely acted upon.[93] To truly dedicate our strength to God, we must embrace our role as proactive servants on the Lord's errand, doing what Christ would do if He were among us. This means purposefully channeling our energy, talents, and resources toward serving others (especially those within our family) and actively pushing back against darkness in whatever forms it may appear. Our life on earth is a precious and quickly passing opportunity, granted for the very purpose of vigorous action—not idle observation or passive belief.

The Lord's rebuke to the early Latter-day Saints underscores this critical principle. He condemned them not merely for unbelief, but explicitly for failing to actively apply and live the truths contained in the Book of Mormon.[94] Mere intel-

93 2 Nephi 2:14, 16, 26.
94 D&C 84:54–57.

lectual assent or passive acknowledgment of gospel principles is insufficient. The gospel is a call to action, requiring real exertion and meaningful effort. Belief without proactive engagement is empty faith. True discipleship demands that we energetically engage in the Lord's work, aligning our physical efforts and spiritual obligations in a unified purpose. Dedicating our strength to God will enable us to more easily rise up above lesser distractions and accomplish the purposes for which we've been placed on earth.

Practical Ideas

Throughout this discussion, we've explored how actively dedicating our heart, soul, mind, and strength to God can empower us to overcome lesser things—distractions, temptations, and false allegiances that can bind us down spiritually and impede our growth. But theory alone isn't enough. Genuine change requires practical application. So let's consider a few concrete, actionable suggestions that can help you consistently apply these principles in your daily life. By intentionally incorporating these practices, you can strengthen your spiritual resilience, sharpen your discernment, and more fully dedicate yourself to God's kingdom.

The Praise of Men

- Begin your day with a meaningful prayer of gratitude. Connect with God and reinforce Him as the guiding influence in your life. Dedicate the day to Him. Ask

Him to help you focus on His approval alone and to see yourself through His eyes. This can help set the tone for the day, reminding you to anchor your identity in Him rather than in the fleeting opinions of others.

- Limit social media and screen time. Social media often fuels the desire for approval and the need to compare ourselves to others. Set daily limits or periodically "fast" from social media to reduce the urge for likes, shares, and followers. Reallocate that time to higher priorities—journaling, studying scripture, recording a religious podcast, or writing a blog post to share your testimony, etc. Better habits can build your identity around God's truths rather than the world's trends.
- Reflect on your day each evening. As part of your nighttime routine, reflect on your actions, decisions, and conversations from that day. Ask yourself questions like, "Did I seek praise or validation from others today? Did I prioritize others' opinions over God's will?" Writing these thoughts down and being brutally honest helps you become more aware of when and why you're seeking worldly approval, so that you can avoid similar traps in the future as you try to give your whole heart to God.

Mammon

- Prioritize tithing. The children of Israel were commanded to give "all the best of the oil, and all the best of the wine, and of the wheat, the firstfruits of them which they shall offer unto the Lord..."[95] The purpose of this practice was so that they would "learn to fear the Lord [their] God always."[96] He was not to be an afterthought—a focus of their charity after the fact. God and His purposes deserved the first and the best. We can also prioritize Him by prioritizing the numerous scriptural injunctions to tithe and give up first what belongs to God to build His kingdom.

- Consecrate. Perhaps fewer scriptures have been so blatantly ignored as those which command us to impart of our substance to the poor. In the modern dispensation, we've been instructed to "remember the poor, and consecrate of thy properties for their support that which thou hast to impart unto them."[97] God's purpose is to prepare a people to return to Him, but "if you will that I give unto you a place in the celestial world, you must prepare yourselves by doing the things which I have commanded you and required of you."[98] One verse prior, he made clear what that is: "For if ye are not equal in earthly things ye cannot be equal in obtaining heavenly things."[99] These are hard truths for people living in a capitalist, individualistic society. But the revelations are explicit: "It is not given

95 Numbers 18:12.
96 Deuteronomy 14:23.
97 D&C 42:30.
98 D&C 78:7.
99 D&C 78:6.

that one man should possess that which is above another, wherefore the world lieth in sin."[100] Give your heart to God by making concerted efforts, without waiting for church direction, to consecrate your belongings. Give freely and frequently to the poor. See yourself as a steward to use these resources both to bless your family's life and others' as well. Build charity into your budget and make it part of your personal and family practice.

- Set financial goals aligned with your spiritual priorities. Consecration does not require living in poverty and giving everything away; one can retain "as much as is sufficient for himself and family."[101] God is, after all, a God of abundance.[102] With what you retain for your family, prudent financial management can allow you to develop and invest your talents[103] in ways aligned with God's values. This doesn't simply mean letting your money sit on autopilot by buying some mutual funds for a long-term retirement plan. It means planning to prioritize what truly matters: spiritual growth through mission trips or charity work; family relationships through travel and meaningful experiences; and service through thoughtful, intentional giving that extends beyond mere monetary contributions. Build a long-term budget that enables you and your family to

100 D&C 49:20.
101 D&C 42:32.
102 2 Corinthians 8:13–14.
103 Matthew 25:14–30.

use your resources for good, both for yourselves and for others.

The Arm of Flesh

- Learn by example. Read scripture stories of faith over human reliance, gaining insight from the experiences of others in order to prepare you to better handle your own. Focus on cases where God's power prevailed over human solutions—like David and Goliath, Daniel in the lion's den, or the faith of the widow of Zarephath. See how God worked in the lives of others, such as the righteous Nephites who submitted themselves to God to protect them from their enemies. Take seriously the counsel of prophets like Nephi, who warned, "cursed is he that putteth his trust in the arm of flesh."[104] You can also learn through bad examples—scrutinizing cases both modern and ancient where people abandoned God's guidance and protection and instead turned to the arm of flesh. Taken together, these stories and circumstances can help give you confidence to better rely on God and give your heart fully to Him.
- Minimize your exposure to secular and social media. Reducing the time you spend consuming these sources of information will decrease your exposure to voices that amplify fear and promote reliance on worldly

104 2 Nephi 4:34.

solutions. Reducing media consumption helps clear mental space for God's voice to guide you instead, allowing faith to replace fear and divine wisdom to inform your perspective. By choosing what you let in, you cultivate a heart tuned to God's truths rather than the shifting narratives of the world.

- Believe Him. When God says that He will fight our battles for us, we ought to pay attention—especially to the conditions listed to deserve that level of protection. For example, when threatened with a physical attack by an enemy, we are commanded to "first lift a standard of peace" and "forgive him," upon which "I, the Lord, would fight their battles."[105] We should not consider these circumstances to be fanciful scriptural tales without modern relevance. God's commands are "an ensemble unto all people, saith the Lord your God, for justification before me."[106] We should seek God's protection and guidance—and believe that He can and will provide it—but doing so requires surrendering our heart and complying with his commandments.

Carnal Desires

- Get an accountability partner. Whatever temptation you might struggle with, the struggle will win over you far more if you fight your battles alone. If you're

105 D&C 98:23–48.
106 D&C 98:38.

enticed by pornography, share your device passwords with your spouse or a trusted person and give your consent to access your device at any time—or use a service like Covenant Eyes to strengthen the accountability even more. If you're wasting time on entertainment or social media, set limits and goals and offer to pay a bonus to your assistant or friend or colleague each time you succeed, so that they're incentivized to help you succeed and hold you accountable. Get creative on how to bring someone into your life to guard your heart from carnal desires.

- Establish a media "fast." A traditional monthly fast focuses on the consumption of food and drink. Create another fast that focuses on content. Choose one day a month—or week—and avoid nonessential media entirely. Use this time to focus on God, family, or other meaningful pursuits that don't involve passive consumption.
- Fill up your idle time. Identify common periods of downtime—perhaps in the evening—when you're most likely to fall into mindless habits or destructive activities, and plan fulfilling alternatives in advance. Carry a book that uplifts you, keep a journal nearby for reflections, or have a project to work on that will easily occupy your time and energy. By consciously filling these moments, you'll be less likely to fall prey to distractions and more focused on things that uplift and draw you closer to God.

Caesar

- Be the change you wish to see in the world. Instead of shirking responsibility for addressing societal problems or delegating that duty to corrupt politicians and bureaucrats, become "anxiously engaged in a good cause, and do many things of [your] own free will, and bring to pass much righteousness."[107] Reject the allure of thinking "someone else ought to fix this," and be part of the solution yourself. Engage in the service that God calls us to,[108] and rise up to help those around you instead of waiting for others to come to their rescue.
- Keep your children out of Caesar's schools. Government-run propaganda mills, commonly called public schools, are petri dishes in which secular and toxic ideas spread. Children are taught to revere the state and its power and pledge allegiance to it. As the Baptist pastor Voddie Baucham once said, "If we continue to send our children to Caesar for their education, we need to stop being surprised when they come home as Romans."[109] By entrusting their formative years to an institution that prioritizes Caesar's values and goals, we are exposing our children to unnecessary spiritual

---

107 D&C 58:27.
108 Mosiah 18:8–9.
109 Voddie Baucham, Jr., "Jurisdictional Boundaries: Who Is Responsible for the Education of Your Child?," in *Indoctrination: Public Schools and the Decline of Christianity* (Green Forest: Master Books, 2012), 263.

combat, leaving them more loyal to the ways of the world than to the ways of God.

- Center the nonaggression principle in your life. This means that initiating force or coercion against others is inherently wrong, except in defense against aggression. It is effectively an extension of the Golden Rule; just as you would not want someone to aggress against you, you should not do so against others. This applies to direct aggression—say, assaulting another person—as well as indirect aggression. Just because you vote for a particular law (that uses coercion to enforce your will on others) or support a tax increase (which uses coercion to take that money from others) doesn't absolve you from the moral responsibility of that threat of force against others. Supporting or endorsing any act that forces others against their will is a violation of the nonaggression principle. Instead of working through Caesar's coercive programs and policies to achieve the outcomes you desire, commit to peaceful solutions, respecting others' autonomy, and refraining from any action—direct or indirect—that would impose upon another person's freedom. In doing so, you align your heart with God's ways of persuasion and love, rejecting the forceful methods of man and embracing the divine principle of agency.

THE KINGDOM TARRIES

In one of his most well-known parables, Jesus likened the kingdom of heaven to ten virgins who traveled to meet the bridegroom—something that sounds foreign to modern ears but was better recognized by Christ's audience. Jewish marital customs involved both a betrothal and a later wedding celebration.[1] Marriage became legally binding at the betrothal, although the bride remained in her father's house during this waiting period, which could last several months or even more than a year. Eventually, the wedding celebration would occur when the bridegroom arrived at the bride's family home to escort her back to his own house or to the location of the feast. When the bridegroom's approach was announced, the young women attending to the bride would go out with their lamps to light his way into the house for the celebration. Because the timing of his arrival was uncertain and typically unannounced, these attendants needed to remain watchful and ready to act at a moment's notice.

John the Baptist was the first to use the bridegroom metaphor to describe Jesus. "I am not the Christ," he told his follow-

1 "Ancient Jewish Marriage," My Jewish Learning, accessed April 12, 2025, https://www.myjewishlearning.com/article/ancient-jewish-marriage/.

ers, "but that I am sent before him. He that hath the bride is the bridegroom: but the friend of the bridegroom, which standeth and heareth him, rejoiceth greatly because of the bridegroom's voice: this my joy therefore is fulfilled."[2] And when these followers later came to Jesus to ask him a question, the Savior used the same metaphor—perhaps to signal to them that He was who John the Baptist had signaled would come: "And Jesus said unto them, Can the children of the bridechamber mourn, as long as the bridegroom is with them? but the days will come, when the bridegroom shall be taken from them..."[3] Later, Paul would portray the relationship between Christ and the church as analogous to marriage,[4] and John would describe Christ's mission in similar marital terms.[5] This recurring bridal metaphor underscores the intimate nature of Christ's connection to His followers, emphasizing devotion, covenantal faithfulness, and eager anticipation.

Jesus reinforced this relational metaphor in his parable—one which shares some interesting insights about how we ought to see ourselves today. Ten virgins prepared to meet the bridegroom and play their part in the celebratory process, yet unexpected delays resulted in the tired women falling asleep.[6] When the call came to meet him, half the virgins found that they had foolishly come ill-prepared and lacked sufficient oil to keep their lamps lit—the precise purpose of their role. They attempted in vain to borrow oil from the

2 John 3:28-29.
3 Matthew 9:15.
4 Ephesians 5:25–27.
5 Revelation 19:7.
6 Matthew 25:5.

others, so they ran to the market to procure some of their own. But upon returning to the bride's home, they found the door shut; the prepared helpers had been invited in, and all others excluded.[7] "Lord, Lord, open to us," they demanded. And then came the bridegroom's stinging reply: "I know you not."[8] Ouch.

Jesus's use of this marital metaphor in the parable reinforces three critical lessons for contemporary followers of Christ. First, it highlights the necessity of personal preparedness: although all ten virgins initially intended to greet the bridegroom, intention alone proved insufficient. Only those who had proactively ensured they had adequate oil—symbolizing spiritual preparation and faithful vigilance—were ready when the critical moment arrived. Second, the parable underscores individual accountability. Each virgin was personally responsible for maintaining her own readiness. Those who attempted at the last moment to borrow preparedness from others discovered a harsh truth: spiritual readiness cannot be quickly obtained from someone else's faithfulness. The wise virgins could not share their oil because readiness requires personal effort and ongoing diligence. Finally, the parable emphasizes the concept of a definitive and irreversible deadline. The bridegroom's arrival marked a clear endpoint; once the door was closed, no latecomers were admitted. The bridegroom's response, with its heavy finality, illustrates that there will ultimately be a moment when opportunities to prepare

---

7 Matthew 25:8–10.
8 Matthew 25:11–12.

will cease, and superficial affiliation without deep devotion will be insufficient.

These lessons are important, but Jesus offers another: "Watch therefore, for ye know neither the day nor the hour wherein the Son of man cometh."[9] As was part of the real-life betrothal experience, the bridegroom in the parable tarried—perhaps for a long time. This deliberate delay is significant. It illustrates that the true test of discipleship is not merely how one prepares for a brief period but how consistently one maintains that preparation over time. The unexpected delay reveals our character and devotion. Many individuals may eagerly embrace faith and the promises of Christ at first, yet the passage of time tests their sincerity, causing some to falter or become complacent.

This was a lesson Jesus emphasized several times when the disciples asked, "What shall be the sign of thy coming, and of the end of the world?"[10] The Savior revealed that "that day and hour knoweth no man, no, not the angels of heaven, but my Father only."[11] And because of the uncertain date of Christ's return—and our impending judgment—His counsel was the same: "Watch therefore: for ye know not what hour your Lord doth come."[12] He continued: "Therefore be ye also ready: for in such an hour as ye think not the Son of man cometh."[13] And, finally, "The lord of that servant shall come in a day when he looketh not for him, and in an hour that he

9 Matthew 25:13.
10 Matthew 24:3.
11 Matthew 24:36.
12 Matthew 24:42.
13 Matthew 24:44.

is not aware of."[14] Taken together, these teachings make clear how important it is for us to cultivate an enduring readiness and active vigilance. Christ intentionally withheld details of His coming not to confuse or frustrate, but to motivate continued discipleship rather than last-minute preparation. The uncertainty of His return is not a call for anxiety but an invitation to live purposefully, intentionally, and faithfully each day.

This extended waiting period raises critical questions for all of us as followers of Christ: Why do He and His kingdom tarry? What unique challenges does this prolonged waiting present? And, most importantly, how must we respond to ensure that we remain vigilant and spiritually prepared? Let's consider the Lord's purposes in delaying His return, the dangers inherent in such waiting, and the deliberate discipleship required to remain faithful through this period of anticipation.

Why the Delay?

At a meeting in Kirtland, Ohio, in 1835, Joseph Smith commented on the Zion's camp journey that had occurred several months prior—a journey that most saw as a failed attempt to redeem Zion and restore the exiled Saints to their homes in Jackson County, Missouri.[15] As documented in the meeting's official minutes, Joseph explained the opportunity the men on this expedition now had:

14 Matthew 24:50.

15 "The Acceptable Offering of Zion's Camp," *Revelations in Context*, The Church of Jesus Christ of Latter-day Saints, https://www.churchofjesuschrist.org/study/manual/revelations-in-context/the-acceptable-offering-of-zions-camp.

> [Joseph] said God had not designed all this for nothing, but he had it in remembrance yet, and those who went to Zion, with a determination to lay down their lives, if necessary, it was the Will of God, that they should be ordained to the ministry and go forth to prune the vineyard for the last time, or the coming of the Lord, which was nigh, even fifty six years, should wind up the scene.[16]

Taken literally, this statement would put the Lord's return in 1891—a date potentially confirmed by an alleged revelation Joseph received after "praying very earnestly to know the time of the coming of the Son of Man." The response he received: "Joseph, my son, if thou livest until thou art eighty-five years old, thou shalt see the face of the Son of Man; therefore let this suffice, and trouble me no more on this matter."[17] Eighty-five years after his 1805 birth would be 1890, only one year off from the prior claim. But Joseph himself seemed uncertain whether this meant much, and the conditional "if" negated the rest of what God said. Joseph, of course, was killed far earlier than his 85th birthday.

What's curious is why Joseph was even bothering to learn and share a date for the Lord's return, since in an 1831 revela-

---

16 "Minutes, Discourse, and Blessings, 14–15 February 1835," Joseph Smith Papers, https://www.josephsmithpapers.org/paper-summary/minutes-discourse-and-blessings-14-15-february-1835/1.

17 D&C 130:14–15; I use the term "alleged" intentionally, as I find William Clayton to be an unreliable source and this claim appears only in his journal. It's also possible this revelation Joseph allegedly referred to in 1843 was the same one referenced in 1835.

tion, the Lord told Joseph that "the hour and the day no man knoweth, neither the angels in heaven, nor shall they know until he comes."[18] No man. No angels. No one would know until the actual coming—Joseph included. But that hasn't stopped speculation from Saints ever since, let alone leaders claiming to know when the great and terrible day would come. Orson Pratt said, "We just as much expect that a city will be built, called Zion, in the place and on the land which has been appointed by the Lord our God, and that a temple will be reared on the spot that has been selected, and the cornerstone of which has been laid, in the generation when this revelation was given."[19] John Taylor claimed to have had an angelic vision in which he saw the world in the year 1945—a world featuring all mountains leveled in a massive earthquake and the constructed Temple of Zion, inhabited by the Lord Himself.[20] Wilford Woodruff predicted the Saints would return to Jackson County to build the great temple in New Jerusalem by 1898.[21] And Lorenzo Snow, two years after that

---

18 D&C 49:7.

19 Orson Pratt, "Order—Spiritual Gifts—Temples—The New Jerusalem," *Journal of Discourses*, vol. 14, https://journalofdiscourses.com/14/38.

20 "ONE HUNDRED YEARS HENCE," Nauvoo Neighbor September 10, 1845, https://archive.org/details/NauvooNeighbor18431845/page/n523/mode/2up. There is no authorial attribution but Taylor was the editor during the paper's entire existence. The vision is sometimes attributed to Parley P. Pratt, who was previously the editor of the *Millennial Star* in which the vision was later published—but no evidence exists for that attribution.

21 Wilford Woodruff, *Journal (October 22, 1865 – December 31, 1872)*, Wilford Woodruff Papers, 145–6. He also predicted, among other things, that the United States would become "so weakened & Broaken to peaces that they called upon Brigham

anticipated date, stated in General Conference as Church president, "Now the time is fast approaching when a large portion of the people that I am now addressing will go back to Jackson County... A large portion of the Latter-day Saints that now dwell in these valleys will go back to Jackson County to build a holy city to the Lord..."[22]

They were all wrong. Perhaps the great anticipation for this culmination of latter-day prophecy was too tempting to remark on, leading people to believe and say things they hoped for but which were not in fact true. The reality is that the bridegroom continues to tarry after all this time, and we continue to wait. Predictions of the Lord's timing by Church leaders are extremely rare in recent history. Most references to the Second Coming simply focus on our need to continue to prepare. "We need to make... spiritual preparation for the events prophesied at the time of the Second Coming," then-Elder Dallin H. Oaks taught in 2004.[23] Elder Neil L. Andersen told young men in 2011 that their future missionary service would "help prepare the world for the Second Coming of the Savior."[24] Eight years later, then-Elder D. Todd Christoffer-

---

Young to take the Presidency of the United States to save the Constitution & the remnant of the Nation from utter destruction."

22 Lorenzo Snow, in *Conference Report*, October 1900, 61, https://archive.org/details/conferencereport1900sa/page/60/mode/2up.

23 Dallin H. Oaks, "Preparation for the Second Coming," April 2004 General Conference, https://www.churchofjesuschrist.org/study/general-conference/2004/04/preparation-for-the-second-coming.

24 Neil L. Andersen, "Preparing the World for the Second Coming," April 2011 General Conference, https://www.churchofjesuschrist.org/study/general-conference/2011/04/preparing-

son said, “It is supremely important to prepare the world for the Second Coming of the Lord Jesus Christ.”[25] And in 2024, President Russell M. Nelson said, “Now is the time for you and for me to prepare for the Second Coming of our Lord and Savior, Jesus the Christ.”[26] One notable exception is from Elder Boyd K. Packer, who in 2011 said to the Church’s youth:

> Sometimes you might be tempted to think as I did from time to time in my youth: “The way things are going, the world’s going to be over with. The end of the world is going to come before I get to where I should be.” Not so! You can look forward to doing it right—getting married, having a family, seeing your children and grandchildren, maybe even great-grandchildren.[27]

Perhaps he’s right, or maybe—like all the others—he’s wrong. After all, “no man knoweth.” But there is danger in buying into the idea that the Lord’s return is some far-off event. When we allow ourselves to believe that Christ’s coming is delayed, our spiritual vigilance may slacken and our readiness deteriorate. We risk falling into complacency, distracted by the mundane tasks and comforts of everyday life. Prolonged waiting tests our faithfulness, creating fertile

---

the-world-for-the-second-coming.

25 D. Todd Christofferson, “Preparing for the Lord’s Return,” April 2019 General Conference, https://www.churchofjesuschrist.org/study/general-conference/2019/04/44christofferson.

26 Russell M. Nelson, “The Lord Jesus Christ Will Come Again,” October 2024 General Conference, https://www.churchofjesuschrist.org/study/general-conference/2024/10/57nelson.

27 Boyd K. Packer, “Counsel to Youth,” October 2011 General Conference, https://www.churchofjesuschrist.org/study/general-conference/2011/10/counsel-to-youth.

ground for doubt, discouragement, or outright dismissal of prophetic warnings.

Is that why the delay exists? "The Lord seeth fit to chasten his people; yea, he trieth their patience and their faith."[28]

The Lord's pending return—and more specifically, the uncertainty of when it will actually occur—serves as a spiritual crucible, refining and revealing the depth of our commitment. God's timeline rarely aligns neatly with human expectations—perhaps intentionally so. Just as the children of Israel spent forty years in the wilderness to humble their hearts and prove their faithfulness, the prolonged period before Christ's return similarly forces us to confront the strength of our devotion when the urgency of immediate expectation fades. Will we continue to diligently cultivate our faith without clear deadlines or immediate rewards? The delay exposes not only our weaknesses but also our true motivations: are we disciples out of fear or convenience, or because we sincerely love and trust God? In this space of uncertainty and prolonged expectation, we are given an opportunity to demonstrate genuine discipleship—choosing faithfulness precisely because it is difficult, uncertain, and demanding.

Perhaps the Lord's deliberate delay of His coming serves a similar purpose as the ancient rites and rituals of the Law of Moses—carefully designed practices intended to keep Israel spiritually focused and away from the pitfalls of idolatry. Constant anticipation of Christ's return can function as a spiritual safeguard, redirecting our thoughts and priorities toward

28 Mosiah 23:21.

heavenly matters. Like the Israelites whose daily observances were intended to remind them of their covenant relationship with God, our ongoing preparation for the Second Coming helps to maintain our spiritual vigilance and readiness. And by consistently living as though Christ could return to Earth at any moment, we simultaneously prepare ourselves for the inevitable encounter with Him at life's end, whether by His return or our own mortality. Preparedness covers both arrivals—the unexpected and the inevitable.

The prolonged wait for Christ's return can also be viewed as an expression of divine mercy—a generous allowance of time granted specifically for repentance and spiritual renewal. Alma emphasized that our mortal existence is "a time granted unto man to repent, yea, a probationary time, a time to repent and serve God."[29] Similarly, Peter taught the early Church that the Lord's apparent delay demonstrates His patient love toward humanity, being "longsuffering to us-ward, not willing that any should perish, but that all should come to repentance."[30] Rather than a passive or arbitrary waiting period, this divine patience actively seeks to provide additional opportunities for individual growth and the gathering of souls into Christ's kingdom. Thus, the Lord's tarrying, seen in this light, is God mercifully extending the window of opportunity for each soul to reconcile with Him.

The kingdom's prolonged tarrying teaches us a vital truth: salvation is not simply a final destination, but an ongoing process of spiritual transformation—a journey where disciple-

---

29 Alma 42:4.
30 2 Peter 3:9.

ship deepens and faith solidifies through patient endurance. Consider Joseph of Egypt, who endured betrayal, slavery, and unjust imprisonment, yet through these prolonged trials, his heart was refined, and his relationship with God matured, preparing him for a divinely appointed mission.[31] Likewise, David's years spent fleeing Saul's wrath were not wasted time but rather formative experiences that shaped him from a shepherd boy into a spiritually strong, humble, and wise leader capable of guiding Israel.[32] These examples illustrate how periods of waiting—though difficult—can mold individuals into more committed and capable servants of God. Similarly, the delay of Christ's return invites each of us to view our spiritual lives as ongoing works in progress, striving for deeper faithfulness and sustained readiness—transforming the waiting itself into sacred preparation.

Delay Difficulties

Sunday morning at your house may be—as it is for so many other families—like orchestrating an Olympic-level event. Shoes mysteriously vanish. Ties become hopelessly tangled. And someone always remembers something—five minutes after they should have left. As dads, we stand by the door issuing calm reminders—calm the first few times, anyway. Patience isn't easy, especially when urgency and timeliness matter. Likewise, waiting on the Lord's timing for His return

31 Genesis 37–41.
32 1 Samuel 18–24.

tests our patience far beyond any frantic Sunday-morning scramble. And the stakes are much higher.

One significant challenge posed by this prolonged waiting period is the loss of a sense of urgency. With Christ's return seemingly forever distant, it can feel like the horizon—always far off, never within reach. This perception can cause spiritual complacency, dulling our sensitivity to the Spirit and softening our resolve. The immediacy that once energized our discipleship gradually fades, replaced by an indifferent attitude that whispers, "I have plenty of time," or "There's always repentance later." Whether we consciously acknowledge it or not, we have embraced a false sense of security, thinking ourselves as having more time before meeting God than we actually might—thus becoming influenced by the adversary:

> And others will he pacify, and lull them away into carnal security, that they will say: All is well in Zion; yea, Zion prospereth, all is well—and thus the devil cheateth their souls, and leadeth them away carefully down to hell.[33]

We *don't* have plenty of time, and there may *not* be repentance later. While the Lord's kingdom may continue to tarry for some time, we could be called home with an unexpected death at any time—even today. Amulek's words are therefore crucial: "I beseech of you that ye do not procrastinate the day of your repentance until the end."[34]

---

33 2 Nephi 28:21.
34 Alma 34:33.

Extended periods of waiting, if not handled well, can lead to spiritual peril. Consider the Israelites who grew impatient when Moses delayed returning from Mount Sinai. Initially fervent in their commitment to God (at least superficially), they quickly descended into idolatry, crafting and worshiping a golden calf.[35] Their prolonged waiting eroded whatever spiritual resolve they may have had and revealed the brittleness of their devotion. Or think of King Saul when facing an imminent Philistine threat. Initially, he waited anxiously for the prophet Samuel to arrive and offer sacrifices. When Samuel delayed, Saul impatiently—and unlawfully—took matters into his own hands, performing the priestly sacrifice himself. This impulsive action, driven by impatience and mistrust in God's timing, led Samuel to deliver a stern rebuke:

> And Samuel said to Saul, Thou hast done foolishly: thou hast not kept the commandment of the Lord thy God, which he commanded thee: for now would the Lord have established thy kingdom upon Israel for ever.
>
> But now thy kingdom shall not continue: the Lord hath sought him a man after his own heart, and the Lord hath commanded him to be captain over his people, because thou hast not kept that which the Lord commanded thee.[36]

Saul's failure to wait well revealed his weak faith and initiated a spiritual decline that would ultimately cost him and

---

35 Exodus 32.

36 1 Samuel 13:13–14.

his family the kingdom. Think also of when Israel, weary of waiting on God's leadership through prophets and judges, instead demanded a human king—someone who could act decisively, whose presence and actions would be visible to all. The Israelites, tempted by this immediacy, desired to be "like all the nations" around them, growing restless under the uncertainty and divine patience required by God's method of direct leadership.[37] The Lord saw clearly what their demand represented: "They have rejected me, that I should not reign over them."[38] Yielding to their impatience led Israel down a path marred by spiritual compromise, political instability, and eventual division and captivity.

Recall, though, how Jesus described the waiting virgins. They were not described as rebellious or obstinate. He didn't say they were idolatrous or impatient. He instead described them as slumbering—falling asleep on the job, as it were.[39] We can't condemn this behavior outright; after all, people need to sleep at some point. Similarly, while the Lord tarries, we have lives to live—running errands, raising children, dealing with disputes, recreating, learning, working, and much more. It's unreasonable to be literally building God's kingdom at all times, focused narrowly and continuously on gospel-oriented tasks to the exclusion of other things that require our attention. We, therefore, necessarily have periods of spiritual slumber where we may be caught a bit off guard were the Lord to return at that exact moment. But this is why Christ's

---

37 1 Samuel 8:5.
38 1 Samuel 8:7.
39 Matthew 25:5.

parable is so interesting—it wasn't just the foolish virgins who slept. All of them did. Thus, the critical test isn't whether our attention occasionally shifts away from the bridegroom, but whether we can swiftly refocus and draw upon the spiritual readiness we've already cultivated.

Yet for men in particular, this readiness can be difficult to sustain precisely because of how we naturally approach goals and responsibilities. We often thrive on clearly defined, tangible objectives, becoming energized when tasks yield immediate and measurable outcomes. The indefinite nature of Christ's return, however, disrupts this default, requiring us to remain spiritually focused without the benefit of visible milestones or definite timelines. Without these clear markers of spiritual progress, maintaining consistent motivation to lead our families and communities can be challenging and exhausting. As a result, the delayed return of the Lord may subtly shift our attention toward achievements that do provide immediate validation—career advancements, professional recognition, and accumulating possessions—gradually overshadowing our spiritual obligations. As should be obvious, then, maintaining readiness demands deliberate effort and regular self-assessment to ensure our spiritual priorities remain front and center, even amid the uncertainty of the bridegroom's return.

Deliberate Discipleship

The extended delay of Christ's return presents unique challenges: maintaining consistent, fervent devotion over decades; safeguarding our testimonies against cynicism or weariness; and consistently prioritizing God's purposes amid daily pressures and the distracting pull of lesser things. Overcoming these challenges demands intentional, sustained effort. How, then, do we as men sustain our spiritual urgency without succumbing to fatigue or complacency?

Christ Himself provided the foundational principle: "Watch therefore: for ye know not what hour your Lord doth come."[40] For men especially, vigilance resonates deeply, as many naturally understand the importance of guarding what they value—be it family, home, or livelihood. Vigilance in our spiritual lives similarly requires active attentiveness and deliberate effort. Christ repeatedly exhorted His disciples to "watch and pray,"[41] underscoring that spiritual vigilance is not passive or infrequent. And without intentional watchfulness, the distractions of daily life will erode our spiritual awareness, leaving us vulnerable to complacency. Too often, well-intentioned Saints drift gradually from the strait and narrow, mistakenly assuming their departure is temporary and return will be easy. This way lies spiritual death.

Active vigilance does not have to cause anxiety or stress. True vigilance is disciplined, balanced, and naturally woven into daily life, uplifting rather than burdening us. Just as regular physical exercise builds endurance and strength, daily spiritual habits like prayer, scripture study, and thoughtful reflection reinforce our spiritual resilience. These practices help us not only endure challenges but flourish spiritually,

40 Matthew 24:42.
41 Matthew 26:41.

despite everyday pressures. Because both physical and spiritual growth often take time to become evident, breaking these processes into manageable, daily actions can provide clear milestones and steady motivation, keeping us committed and encouraged.

However, spiritual disciplines should never become just items to check off a list. For many men, there's a tendency to compartmentalize faith, restricting it mostly to Sundays or church activities. We have our "Sunday bucket" and then the rest of our time is just that—ours—for sports, work, projects, family, and more. But genuine discipleship requires a broader and more integrated approach. Christ said to "seek ye first the kingdom of God, and his righteousness."[42] This means having a spiritual focus for every aspect of our lives—our work decisions, family relationships, financial choices, and personal goals. Adopting this holistic approach helps us align our daily activities with eternal goals. Far from limiting our effectiveness or enjoyment, living this way enhances both by giving greater meaning and purpose to everything we do. Not only does it prepare us for whenever the Lord comes again (or when we die and return to Him), but it also improves our daily life and enriches our relationships on a daily basis.

Shifting from passive waiting to proactive preparation is especially critical for men who naturally thrive on initiative and action. Christ's return isn't merely something we await; it is something we actively prepare for each day. Passivity makes us vulnerable, while proactive preparation cultivates

42 Matthew 6:33.

spiritual strength and resilience. Consider spiritual preparedness as you might physical conditioning: regular, intentional effort builds spiritual endurance and readiness. True discipleship develops stamina—a rhythm of steady faith that outlasts long stretches of apparent divine silence. Abraham waited a quarter-century for Isaac;[43] the brother of Jared lingered four long years on the seashore before the Lord finally spoke;[44] the early Saints in Missouri and Nauvoo died without seeing Zion redeemed. Their histories confirm that God often refines men through delay. We tread the same path: the kingdom tarries, and the very slowness of its advance can feel like a weight on our backs. What, then, does deliberate discipleship look like when heaven seems quiet?

Own the Watch, Don't Clock Out. Ancient sentinels rotated through the night in three-hour watches. If even one guard dozed, the whole camp was exposed. Likewise, spiritual vigilance cannot be "on" during conference weekend and "off" the rest of the year. Establish fixed "watch hours" in your calendar—a sunrise study block, a midday gratitude pause, an evening self-reflection. These scheduled check-ins train the heart to stay awake.[45] Consistency, not duration, forges alertness: a focused ten-minute scripture session seven days a week outperforms an occasional marathon that leaves you spiritually exhausted and otherwise dormant.

43 Genesis 21:5; Hebrews 6:15.
44 Ether 2:13–14.
45 Mark 13:35–37.

Convert Waiting Time into Working Time. While Noah awaited rain, he built.[46] While Nephi awaited further instructions, he forged tools.[47] Waiting is not an intermission—it is an assignment. Identify projects that push the kingdom forward now: mentoring another, teaching your children self-reliance skills, starting a community service project, or drafting a neighborhood emergency plan. Proactive labor transforms hazy anticipation into measurable progress and prevents the cynicism that idleness breeds.[48]

Practice the Lord's Return. Complacency thrives when the Second Coming feels abstract. Bridge that distance by holding a regular personal review: *If Christ returned tonight, what would I wish I'd finished, repented of, or taught my family?* Write the answers, then tackle one item each week. This exercise resets priorities and injects a bit of holy urgency without morbid fear.[49]

Anticipate Mockers and Manage the Noise. Peter foresaw a last-days chorus of scoffers sneering, "Where is the promise of his coming?"[50] Lehi witnessed the same spirit in the great and spacious building, its occupants "mocking and pointing their fingers" at those pressing toward the tree of life.[51] Centuries later, unbelievers in Zarahemla set a fixed day to

---

46 Genesis 7:10; Hebrews 11:7.
47 1 Nephi 17:9–11, 16.
48 D&C 58:27.
49 Alma 34:32–33.
50 2 Peter 3:3–4.
51 1 Nephi 8:26–27.

slaughter the faithful if the prophesied sign of Christ's birth failed to appear.[52] Mockery is, therefore, a covenant-era constant—today it just wears earbuds and streams on repeat. So limit intake of voices that seek to erode our faith. When exposure is unavoidable, respond by doubling down on commitment to deliberate discipleship. Quiet obedience speaks to heaven—and to your own soul—far louder than any argument fired across a screen.

Deliberate discipleship, then, is disciplined vigilance married to purposeful action. It is the daily choice to keep the lamp trimmed long after midnight has passed and the street appears empty, confident that the bridegroom is nearer now than when we first believed. Each dawn offers a fresh post on the watchtower, where men of God striving to rise up can scan the horizon while hammering nails into ark-building projects the world can neither see nor value. In this long obedience, the waiting itself becomes sanctifying: muscles of faith thicken, spiritual reflexes sharpen, compassion deepens, and the taste for lesser things grows dull. Day by steady day, spiritual calluses form where once there was softness, enabling hands to grip the iron rod even when storms howl and popular opinion mocks.

---

52 3 Nephi 1:9.

THE DAY OF BROTHERHOOD

I imagine Helaman's sandals scuffing through the dust as he moved down the ragged line after a ferocious battle—one, two, three... a thousand... fifteen hundred—his heartbeat climbing with every count. When dawn broke, two thousand stripling volunteers had sprinted toward a seasoned Lamanite army that outmassed and outmaneuvered them. They were likely farmhands, not fighters; their swords no doubt still smelled of newly polished bronze. Logic demanded stretchers and body bags. Instead, as Helaman reached the final cluster of youth, his stunned tally confirmed the impossible: "there was not one soul of them who did perish."[1]

Why? The record gives the secret in a single phrase—they fought "with exactness... according to their faith."[2] Exactness is not rigidity; it is perfect alignment. Two thousand wills welded to a covenant forged first in the hearts of their mothers, then sealed in their own.[3] Every thrust, every shield-lift, every exertion to defend themselves seemingly moved like synchronized muscle fibers in a single body. Heaven magni-

---

1 Alma 57:25.
2 Alma 57:21.
3 Ibid.

fied what hell could not fracture: covenant brothers acting as one.

That miracle is more than battlefield lore—it is a blueprint for a latter-day "day of brotherhood." Because our enemies, though subtler, are no less lethal. Pornographic algorithms, tribal politics, and spiritual apathy slice at modern men with the same intent: sever them from covenant purpose. The result is spiritual death by a thousand proverbial paper cuts. But today, many quorums—would-be units of brotherhood—resemble scattering skirmishers, each goodhearted but isolated. They're sparks, to be sure, but too far apart to kindle a blaze.

Even our hymnbook seems to nudge us toward Helaman's secret. Where Merrill originally penned, "His kingdom tarries long," a line that kept eyes glued to an unarriving dawn, later hymnals traded delay for unity: "in one united throng." Thus, the stanza became (and remains in the Church's hymnal):[4]

> *Rise up, O men of God,*
> *In one united throng.*
> *Bring in the day of brotherhood*
> *and end the night of wrong.*

The editors shifted the spotlight from when Christ comes to how we stand while He tarries. Immediately after, the hymn commands, "Bring in the day of brotherhood." The line

---

4 Though the Church's hymnal cites William Merrill as the author of the lyrics for "Rise Up, O Men of God," it does not admit to any alteration. In addition to this changed line, Merrill's third stanza is omitted entirely. More on that later in the book.

is a trumpet note: stop watching the clock and start gathering the workers. A solitary craftsman can rough out a stone, but it takes a crew to raise a temple spire. Time itself quickens when we shift into action—purpose has a way of shortening the wait. The School of the Prophets compressed doctrinal growth that might have taken decades into a single winter because every mind in that small loft bent toward one question: How do we serve the Lord together? Zion's Camp left only a few graves on Missouri soil, yet from its ranks came nearly every future apostle, bonded by blistered feet and shared prayers. Then came the forty-year labor on the Salt Lake Temple: quarrymen chiseling granite in a canyon twenty miles away, teamsters ferrying ten-ton blocks across mud and snow, sisters donating homemade clothing so stonecutters could stay on the payroll. When the capstone finally settled into place, it embodied thousands of quiet consecrations mortared together into a single act of worship.

These stories reveal a sort of divine arithmetic: scattered effort adds, but united effort multiplies—and in multiplying, it lifts men above the gravitational pull of lesser things. When brotherhood takes hold, rival schedules and interests loosen their grip. The question shifts from "What do I have time for?" to "What does the kingdom need?" Disagreements shrink beside a common altar, and what began as sacrifice soon feels like privilege because every hour and dollar consecrated becomes another stone in Zion's wall, another proof that ordinary men can rise up and trade the transient for the eternal.

The stripling miracle is, therefore, not trapped in scripture's amber; it is waiting for repetition. It will not be achieved by louder slogans or lonelier effort, but by men aligning hearts the way craftsmen true a beam, each small adjustment bringing the structure into perfect plumb. When that alignment is complete, heaven will do again what it did for Helaman's youth—amplify mortal strength until the outcome defies the odds and even the weary counters must admit, with wonder, that not one soul is lost.

Covenant Brotherhood

The house in Capernaum was already thick with bodies when the four friends arrived, each corner of their makeshift litter digging into a different shoulder. They had carried the paralytic through the narrow streets at dawn, optimistic that somehow they would squeeze him into Christ's presence. But the doorway was jammed, the windows blocked by spectators pressing for a glimpse of Galilee's new Teacher. It would have been easy—reasonable, even—to postpone the errand for a future, quieter day. Instead, the men climbed the outer stair to the flat roof, knelt in the dust, and began removing the tiles. Falling debris no doubt drew gasps from below as sunlight pierced the interior's darkness. Ropes were tied, a stretcher eased down, and suddenly the sick man lay at the Savior's feet. Luke chooses his words with deliberate precision: Jesus "saw their faith" and declared, "Man, thy sins are forgiven thee... arise, take up thy bed, and go unto thine house."[5] The miracle announced a principle as stunning as the

5 Luke 5:20, 24; Matthew 9:2, 6; Mark 2:1–12.

healing itself: heaven's power descends most readily on faith forged in common cause.

That vignette is an ideal entry point to the subject of priesthood brotherhood, because it highlights three truths that continue to govern God's work among men. First, divine power is not a personal trophy case; it is a shared stewardship. Second, that power is animated only by relational virtues—"by persuasion, by long-suffering, by gentleness and meekness, and by love unfeigned."[6] None of them functions in isolation. A man can memorize a manual by himself; he cannot practice these virtues without another human being. Third, when those virtues converge in collective action, ordinary effort is multiplied into extraordinary impact. Moses learned that on a hill overlooking Israel's skirmish with Amalek. As long as his arms held the rod aloft, the Israelites advanced, but fatigue set in, and the line began to falter. "Moses' hands were heavy; and [Aaron and Hur] took a stone, and put it under him, and he sat thereon; and [they] stayed up his hands, the one on the one side, and the other on the other side; and his hands were steady until the going down of the sun." Victory was recorded for Israel's army, but it hinged on three men acting as one.[7]

Latter-day Saint history is thick with similar examples of brotherly action. In 1833 a few dozen elders packed into a low-ceilinged loft in Kirtland, fasting, washing one another's feet, and grappling with questions that would later be canonized.[8] The School of the Prophets lasted a matter of months,

---

6 D&C 121:41.
7 Exodus 17:8–13.
8 The resulting Lectures on Faith, included in the 1835 Doctrine

yet the doctrine clarified there and the missions launched from that room carried the gospel across an ocean and deeper into the Saints' hearts. That same collective muscle lifted three early temples: in Kirtland, Nauvoo, and later Salt Lake City; lay Saints quarried stone, hauled timber, and traded labor tithing—working every tenth day on the temple without pay. The result was a sacred space none could have financed or built alone. Zion's Camp in 1834 marched more than 200 men on a 1,800-mile round trip through mud, flood, and cholera—not to win back land (they never did) but to forge a leadership corps who learned under hardship to trust God and one another. And when early blizzards trapped the Martin and Willie handcart companies in 1856, those same instincts sparked a valley-wide rescue: farmers left harvests uncut, hitched teams overnight, and trudged through snow to carry starving emigrants across the Sweetwater River, many surrendering their own blankets and boots. Doctrine clarified, stone set upon stone, future apostles steeled for later trials, and hundreds of lives preserved—all because priesthood holders treated a neighbor's burden as their own. Again and again, the record shows that heaven's power descends most readily on shoulders lifting in unison.

Fast forward to the present. Those men who faithfully attend worship services find predictable processes, neatly planned with quorum meetings relying on regurgitated conference talks and superficial sharing from those few who choose to engage. Activities—if they're planned at all—draw

---

and Covenants, were later removed in 1921.

more sighs than signups, and service projects struggle to assemble enough helpers to matter. The ministering program tries to bridge the gaps, but assigned pairs and perfunctory texts simply cannot rival the strength of social cohesion built upon natural friendships between neighbors. Brotherhood thrives where a knock on the door needs no reminder, where men spot a need and step in before anyone asks, where covenant ties turn proximity into responsibility. Until that spirit is common again, the vehicle of priesthood fellowship will remain parked, its potential power idling unused.

The need is urgent because, as Merrill's hymn says, a "night of wrong" closes in: addictions that flourish in secrecy, marriages crumbling under silent strain, families struggling under a mountain of debt while neighbors assume things are fine. Darkness thrives in isolation. A man who believes he must fight alone usually surrenders somewhere between exhaustion and despair; a man connected to others may stumble but is far harder to keep down. The next chapter will examine that contest in detail. For now, it is enough to mark the front line. Wherever men of God see another's burden and treat it as their own, night gives way to morning light. The four roof-ripping friends did not wait for permission or title. They saw a blocked door, thought together, and made another way in. That is still the pattern. Learn your duty, spot the brother who cannot make the journey alone, and grab the corner nearest your hand. The Lord continues to respond to collective faith, and power still follows when His sons act in concert.

The deeper the night of wrong, the more urgently the Lord needs the solidarity of saintly men united in purpose. Darkness does not typically yield to solitary effort; it recoils when godly voices and hands combine. Think of Gideon, who faced the Midianite host with only three hundred soldiers, yet prevailed because every man kept his torch aloft and his trumpet ready. Numbers are less important than the unity of purpose that turns scattered resolve into a single strike. Satan understands this arithmetic perfectly. If he can keep priesthood holders distracted, discouraged, disengaged, or divided, opposition to his plans remains weak. Ezra Taft Benson warned of that very strategy:

> The devil knows that if the elders of Israel should ever wake up, they could step forth and help preserve freedom and extend the gospel. Therefore the devil has concentrated, and to a large extent successfully, in neutralizing much of the priesthood. He has reduced them to sleeping giants.[9]

This warning has not been sufficiently heeded. Too many elders drift through meetings, scroll through phones, and consider discipleship as doing the bare minimum to follow the "active member" checklist. That is what "neutralized" looks like—muscle that never strains and faith that never leaves the chair. We reverse that only by treating our priesthood like any serious job: know the objective, divide the tasks, and follow through until the work is finished. Each quorum should be able to name the brother it is helping back to activity, the family it is lifting out of financial trouble, and the person whose

9 Ezra Taft Benson, *God, Family, Country: Our Three Great Loyalties* (Salt Lake City: Deseret Book Company, 1974), 385–89.

home they'll be doing a service project at that Saturday. Progress requires intentionality, not vague desire, unplanned. Real brotherhood is built in these straightforward ways—show up, plan, act, report, and repeat—by men who commit, coordinate, and complete. Until that becomes normal, we will keep good intentions and lose battles we should win.

Unity Without Sameness

Benson's picture of a neutralized priesthood—giants asleep on the job—calls for more than a loud alarm. We first have to "awake, and arise from the dust,"[10] ready to "put on the armor of righteousness" and shake off every chain that limits our usefulness.[11] Nowhere in this process of awakening and action, however, are we called to conform. That we are commanded by Christ to "be one"[12]—or in Merrill's words, "one united throng"—does not mean we must be the same. Quite the opposite: the brotherhood of man is stronger because of its diverse range of backgrounds and abilities.

Israel had been out of Egypt only a few months when the Lord issued an audacious command to the children of Israel: "Let them make me a sanctuary; that I may dwell among them."[13] In a desert camp of former slaves—people with no permanent homes and no stable supply chain—Moses was to construct an ornate, portable temple worthy of God's presence. The specifications were exacting: frames of acacia wood

10 Moroni 10:31.
11 2 Nephi 1:23.
12 D&C 38:27.
13 Exodus 25:8.

overlaid with gold, curtains woven from scarlet and blue linen, loops of bronze and clasps of silver, an ark topped by hammered cherubim. Where would nomads in Sinai find such wealth and craftsmanship? The need was urgent; Israel's covenant identity now hinged on a place where the Lord could meet them.

Moses gathered the congregation and issued a call for both materials and skill. The response was immediate and varied. Leaders brought onyx stones, women spun goat hair, and willing-hearted men and women offered bracelets, earrings, rings, and other jewels of gold.[14] Artisans were "filled... with the spirit of God, in wisdom, in understanding, and in knowledge" to design, engrave, weave, and set jewels.[15] Others learned and worked under their direction. Day after day the offerings piled so high that Moses finally had to proclaim, "Let neither man nor woman make any more work for the offering of the sanctuary" because "the stuff they had was sufficient."[16] Metalworkers, carpenters, weavers, perfumers, and donors of every stripe meshed their distinct resources until the tabernacle stood complete—proof that a single sacred project can draw on a broad band of talents, each indispensable, none sufficient alone.

Paul spelled out this principle to the Corinthians. "For the body is not one member, but many," he wrote, listing hands, ears, eyes, and feet, each directed by a single head.[17] An eye

14 Exodus 35:21–29.
15 Exodus 35:30–35.
16 Exodus 36:5–7.
17 1 Corinthians 12:14–21.

by itself can't walk; a foot alone can't read road signs. Healthy function requires parts that do different things in coordinated rhythm. Our modern quorums, and the army of priesthood more broadly, is no different. When everyone in the room has the same background, the same knowledge, and the same talents, the group hits its ceiling quickly. Builders, teachers, entrepreneurs, accountants, lawyers, daily laborers, and countless more—each brings a gift the next man lacks, and the Church needs the full catalog. The goal, as Paul said, is "that there should be no schism in the body; but that the members should have the same care one for another."[18]

We are meant to be both varied and united—a seeming paradox that mirrors the Godhead itself. The Father and the Son are distinct beings, yet perfectly "one" in purpose and will.[19] Our charge is similar: preserve individuality while aligning intentions. Unity in this sense is not an exercise in cloning; it draws strength precisely because backgrounds, skills, and viewpoints differ. As D. Todd Christofferson said, "Unity does not require sameness, but it does require harmony. We can have our hearts knit together in love, be one in faith and doctrine, and still cheer for different teams, disagree on various political issues, debate about goals and the right way to achieve them, and many other such things."[20] When a quorum blends a contractor's eye for structure, a teacher's gift for explanation, and a counselor's instinct to listen, the

---

18 1 Corinthians 12:14–21.

19 D&C 93:3; 3 Nephi 11:27.

20 D. Todd Christofferson, "One in Christ," April 2023 General Conference, https://www.churchofjesuschrist.org/study/general-conference/2023/04/41christofferson.

result is smarter plans and sturdier people than any single talent could produce. Difference, properly harnessed, is not the enemy of unity—it is the engine that drives it.

Imagine your quorum devoting one Sunday to an inventory of sorts. Each brother lists trade skills, professional expertise, tools he's willing to lend, assets he has available for use, and spiritual gifts he feels prompted to share. One line might read, "Licensed electrician, owns a truck and 24-foot ladder, gift of discernment." Another: "CPA, fluent in Spanish, laptop lab with ten spare Chromebooks." A simple spreadsheet could be maintained to keep track of what each has to offer. Add the Relief Society's many possible contributions—nursing credentials, meal-prep capacity, gardening savvy, language fluency, and more—and suddenly the ward owns a real-time map of resources far richer than any single leader's fleeting memory. One can imagine Moses gladly trading a sandstone tablet for a list like this; when contributions are inventoried, small offerings can compound into producing great things quickly.[21]

This diversity of abilities makes the matching almost automatic when a need surfaces. A newly arrived family facing tax problems is paired with the CPA before Sunday ends; a widow's faulty breaker box is routed to the electrician; a missionary headed to Colombia spends Wednesday nights with the Spanish speakers. Fast response deepens trust, and trust encourages even broader participation: the brother who once felt he had nothing to offer sees how his welding rig or knack for résumé editing fills a gap and helps another. Needs turn

21 Alma 37:6–7.

into ministry opportunities, ministry turns into fellowship, and the ward begins to run on the quiet power of members succoring one another in meaningful ways.

Therein lies the key to unity among a diverse people—linking givers and receivers, each offering what he possesses. To the Corinthian Saints, Paul framed it this way: "Now therefore perform the doing of it; that as there was a readiness to will, so there may be a performance also out of that which ye have. For if there be first a willing mind, it is accepted according to that a man hath, and not according to that he hath not."[22] The contribution God accepts is the one you can actually lay on the table—time if you lack means, labor if you lack money, listening if you lack tools. Heaven does not tally what is missing from a man's inventory; it reckons the value of what he willingly brings.

Paul then anticipated a common worry: Does the obligation to consecrate what we have for the building of God's kingdom leave Saints burdened while others coast? "I mean not that other men be eased, and ye burdened," Paul wrote.[23] The perception is entirely wrong; men of God who rise up and are of service to others are not "burdened" while others are "eased" with their inaction or being beneficiaries of others' work. Quite the opposite. Paul revealed that this, in fact, is a path to equality: "that now at this time your abundance may be a supply for their want, that their abundance also may be a supply for your want."[24] One household's surplus grain covers another's empty pantry; another day, the rescued family supplies gratitude,

---

22 2 Corinthians 8:11–12.
23 2 Corinthians 8:13.
24 2 Corinthians 8:14.

loyalty, and future service when roles reverse. Material help moves one direction, spiritual dividends return the other, until wants and abundances trade places often enough that everyone experiences both giving and receiving. Properly understood, this exchange does not foster dependence; it forges solidarity, proving that variety in assets and abilities is the very mechanism God uses to knit His people into one.

Diverse men rising up together to create equality and unity through their different offerings becomes a safeguard against the discouragement President Benson described. Sleeping giants often stay asleep because they assume another individual or institution will handle the need. But once we see that every gift counts, excuses fade. As we offer our unique skills and services, temporal or spiritual, then momentum builds, habits form, and the adversary's plan to neutralize priesthood effort hits resistance. The thesis is simple: the Lord built diversity into His Church on purpose. When we waste that resource by encouraging conformity to a homogenous standard or style, we shrink the Church's capacity. When we harness it, we unlock power that no single talent could achieve. That combination is what the day of brotherhood needs most in order to combat the night of wrong: many kinds of men, moving in one direction, producing results none could manage alone and few could have predicted.

Priesthood in Action

The wilderness tabernacle that the children of Israel constructed was more than ancient history for the early Latter-day Saints; it was the pattern they consciously reenacted. In Kirtland, farmers who barely scraped by donated labor tithing—every tenth day on scaffolds instead of in fields. At Nauvoo, laborers and artisans alike hauled and dressed limestone, framed intricate woodwork, and then worked by torchlight after regular shifts to lift the temple walls steadily skyward. In Salt Lake, the sacrifice spanned four decades with a steady stream of granite blocks hewn in Little Cottonwood Canyon and ox teams bogged in the mud. The price in time, talent, and treasure was staggering, but so was the payoff—a holy space to commune with the Lord.

That same ethic carried over to local meetinghouses. Well into the twentieth century, wards organized construction committees, pooled savings, raised funds, and volunteered time to build new chapels for their worship services. Because nearly every family had a brick, beam, or dollar personally invested, the finished chapels felt less like dispassionate space that simply existed and more like an extension of home—rooms that carried the scent of personal sacrifice and therefore invited reverence the moment the doors opened. They had an ownership stake in the success—and use—of these spaces.

Today, Church members only indirectly contribute to the building of sacred spaces—and even then, only financially. We are now far removed from the process, with professionals in charge of each step. The modern system makes obvious practical sense. With congregations sprouting across six continents, a centralized building program can purchase materials in bulk, hire specialists who understand seismic codes and local regulations, and finish dozens of chapels in the time it once took a single ward to pour footings. Members whose schedules leave little room for night-shift construction can donate money instead and still see a meetinghouse rise on time and under budget. Efficiency has soared—but not without other costs. Without having a stake in the final result—and participating in the process of its creation—we surrender the layers of memory that come from mixing concrete next to a brother or sanding pews with a son. Over time, we may begin to view every kingdom project the same way: the Church will plan it, tithing reserves will fund it, contractors will build it, and someone else will staff it. The institutional Church becomes the default problem-solver, and personal ownership and individual action quietly erodes.

That drift is dangerous. I'm not necessarily advocating that we must return to individual members building their own chapels, but rather warning of what can happen if we acclimatize ourselves to this process of relying on the institution over our individual involvement. We know that the Lord condemns "slothful servants" who wait "to be commanded in all things," warning that such hesitation earns "no reward."[25] If we train ourselves to assume that Church budgets and programs will cover every need, we risk silencing personal revelation and shrinking the reach of our own gifts. A kingdom built by professionals alone would run smoothly—and lack the very discipleship that sanctifies its builders. Our charge, I think, is to reverse the slide: see, step in, and lift where we stand.[26]

25 D&C 58:26–29.

26 Dieter F. Uchtdorf, "Lift Where You Stand," October 2008 Gen-

We act first because our covenants obligate us to be agents who, instead of being acted upon, decide to act.[27] The difference between the two approaches—acting agents anxiously engaged versus slothful servants turned spectators—defines whether our brotherhood rises up to become a living force or slips back down into the slumber President Benson feared.

The Church already offers plenty of entry points for hands-on service. A member can spend time working at a welfare farm, log on to JustServe to find a local project, or don on a yellow Helping Hands vest after a hurricane. Missionaries at Welfare Square, bishops' storehouses, and employment centers devote full-time effort to lifting others, supported by others formally called part-time to offer consistent support. These programs prove that institutional resources are real and ready. They are not, however, meant to absorb everything the Lord wants done. It is dangerous to think that because a program exists, our personal obligation is somehow satisfied. It is easy to reason that if something critical were missing, the bishop would call us—and then slip back to the comfort of schedules and screens. Easy, yes—but also slothful and spiritually destructive.

So the real measuring stick for any priesthood quorum is not how many assignments are received but how many needs are noticed and met before an assignment becomes necessary. A kingdom built on that culture will never run short of projects, testimonies, or miracles—and the giants President

---

eral Conference, https://www.churchofjesuschrist.org/study/general-conference/2008/10/lift-where-you-stand.

27 2 Nephi 2:26.

Benson described will be fully awake, working side by side in the light of day.

That kind of self-starting culture matters for more than the immediate project list; it is what our children will use to gauge what discipleship looks like (and whether it's something they want to embrace as adults). They sit in the same meetings we do, hear the same counsel, and quickly spot the gap between talk and follow-through. If they grow up experiencing a passive people who slothfully wait until a formal calling or request is extended before doing anything, they will learn that good intentions without corresponding actions are acceptable. Recall that the Saints remain under condemnation until we not only talk the talk but also walk the walk.[28] Too many honor God with their lips, but their hearts—and their resulting actions—are far from Him.[29] Our example—far more than our words—teaches the rising generation whether God's commandments are warnings to heed or slogans to substantively ignore. Modeling unscripted service is the surest way to raise future Saints who treat God's kingdom as their personal responsibility rather than as headquarters' job. There are plenty of "traditions of the fathers" that should be avoided. Our opportunity is to develop righteous traditions that, if emulated, will empower our posterity to take action and grow God's kingdom.

---

28 D&C 84:57.
29 Matthew 15:8–9.

THE NIGHT OF WRONG

The prince of darkness was once a beacon of light. Lucifer—literally "light bearer" or "morning star"—walked in God's glory for ages, yet repackaged darkness so persuasively that vast numbers found it appealing. Before he was "thrust down from the presence of God,"[1] Lucifer first persuaded "a third part"[2] of God's children to unite with him. His sales line was blunt: Follow me and I will guarantee salvation. It was a consequence-free plan—one in which participants could "eat, drink, and be merry,"[3] with no regard for the wrongness of their actions, as Lucifer claimed he would (somehow) "redeem all mankind."[4]

The "war in heaven" was a civil conflict among God's spirit children, each camp championing a competing plan. Heavenly Father's plan, upheld by Christ, would affirm agency and allow people to make wrong choices and suffer the consequences. Justice required a Redeemer: Christ would atone for sin, enabling believers to repent and regain God's presence. By contrast, Lucifer's alternative proposal "sought to destroy the agency of man"[5] by eliminating consequences of their

1 D&C 76:25.
2 D&C 29:36.
3 2 Nephi 28:7–8.
4 Moses 4:1.
5 Moses 4:3.

choices and saving everyone. As Joseph Smith put it, "Jesus said there would be certain souls that would not be saved, and the devil said he could save them all; the grand council gave in for Jesus Christ: so the devil rebelled against God and fell, and all who put up their heads for him."[6]

Following his fall, Lucifer "became Satan, yea, even the devil, the father of all lies, to deceive and to blind men."[7] But this was not a new role; it was a continuation of the stratagem he had previously employed. The war in heaven would continue, simply moving to a new battlefield. But God didn't want His children ill-equipped for the battle, having passed through a veil of forgetfulness and thus not remembering how this fallen son and his followers acted. Through prophets, God warned us of the motives of and methods used by these dark spirits. "There are many spirits which are false spirits," the Lord once revealed, "which have gone forth in the earth, deceiving the world. And also Satan hath sought to deceive you, that he might overthrow you."[8] Over and over again, God points out "a pattern in all things, that [we] may not be deceived."[9] He provides us with spiritual gifts "that [we] may not be deceived."[10] Truth, for Him, is paramount. Truth is His glory.[11]

---

6 Discourse, 7 April 1844, as Published in *Times and Seasons*, Joseph Smith Papers, accessed May 18, 2025, https://www.josephsmithpapers.org/paper-summary/discourse-7-april-1844-as-published-in-times-and-seasons/5.

7 Moses 4:4; Revelation 12:9.

8 D&C 50:2–3.

9 D&C 52:14.

10 D&C 46:8.

11 D&C 93:36.

Through his mortal minions, Satan employs deception to compromise the faithful and bind them with flaxen cords.[12] The Book of Mormon is especially clear in demonstrating this trend, from Zeezrom and the Zoramites to Amalickiah, Nehor, Korihor, and more. Deception is Satan's primary tool, always aimed at prying humankind away from God. But an outright appeal to spiritual alienation is not itself appealing; confrontation often creates resistance. Hence Satan whispers, "There is no hell… I am no devil, for there is none."[13] His methods are more sinister and subtle than direct. He appeals to the carnal man's desires for power and wealth. And the promise is the same as it was in the premortal realm: to "eat, drink, and be merry"[14]—to acquire and enjoy the benefits of worldly power and wealth—without apparent consequence. Thus, when the secret combinations spread throughout society they felt free to "murder, and plunder, and steal, and commit whoredoms and all manner of wickedness" since they had obtained sufficient political power to operate not by God's law or civil law but by "the laws of their wickedness."[15] Once they "usurped the power and authority of the land" they "[let] the guilty and the wicked go unpunished because of their money," empowering themselves "to rule and do according to their wills, that they might get gain and glory of the world, and, moreover, that they might the more easily commit adultery, and steal, and kill, and do according to their own wills."[16] The promise of

---

12 2 Nephi 26:22.
13 2 Nephi 28:22.
14 2 Nephi 28:7–8.
15 Helaman 6:23–24.
16 Helaman 7:4–5.

power and wealth—and the ability to avoid the consequences of one's actions—was just as seductive to the Nephites[17] as it was to a third part of God's children eons ago. It is no less seductive today.

Yet the claim that the guilty can sin with impunity is itself the master deceit. Truth and consequence may be delayed, but they cannot be escaped. "Whatsoever is truth is light," the Lord declares.[18] Light exposes; sooner or later, it will punch through every shadow where Satan operates. Conspiring people therefore labor in darkness—in Isaiah's words, "They seek deep to hide their counsel."[19] Not even nine months after the Church's reorganization, the Lord identified them as "the enemy in the secret chambers."[20] Moroni warned that if we allow such works of darkness to spread, "it shall be the cause of the destruction of all people."[21] Ignoring such forces today simply provides them more room to grow.

This corrupt condition—this conspiracy to seek after and exploit power and wealth to the detriment of others, particularly the righteous[22]—is the night of wrong. When light is absent, justice stalls, agency shrivels, and entire cultures drift into moral sleep. When the Saints were persecuted and incarcerated, they keenly felt these effects. From his jail cell in Liberty, Missouri, Joseph Smith wrote of "the most damning hand of murder, tyranny, and oppression, supported and

17 Helaman 6:38.
18 D&C 84:45.
19 Isaiah 29:15.
20 D&C 38:28.
21 Ether 8:22.
22 Helaman 6:39; 7:5.

urged on and upheld by the influence of that spirit which hath so strongly riveted the creeds of the fathers, who have inherited lies, upon the hearts of the children, and filled the world with confusion, and has been growing stronger and stronger, and is now the very mainspring of all corruption, and the whole earth groans under the weight of its iniquity."[23] He suggested compiling records of all these injustices to expose the conspiring acts of wicked people—"not only publish to all the world, but present them to the heads of government in all their dark and hellish hue, as the last effort which is enjoined on us by our Heavenly Father, before we can fully and completely claim that promise which shall call him forth from his hiding place; and also that the whole nation may be left without excuse before he can send forth the power of his mighty arm."[24]

This effort to expose darkness was, in Joseph's mind, "an imperative duty" for Latter-day Saints—one that "we owe to all the rising generation, and to all the pure in heart."[25]

> For there are many yet on the earth among all sects, parties, and denominations, who are blinded by the subtle craftiness of men, whereby they lie in wait to deceive, and who are only kept from the truth because they know not where to find it—
>
> Therefore, that we should waste and wear out our lives in bringing to light all the hidden things of darkness,

23 D&C 123:7.
24 D&C 123:6.
25 D&C 123:11.

> wherein we know them; and they are truly manifest from heaven—
>
> These should then be attended to with great earnestness. Let no man count them as small things; for there is much which lieth in futurity, pertaining to the saints, which depends upon these things.[26]

Ending the night starts by switching on the light and naming the darkness. We are to *waste and wear out our lives* bringing these dark acts to the light of day. This is the point of the day of brotherhood—to be that very light. We are to reclaim, with God's truth, those who are blinded by deceptive spirits and their mortal minions. Our task, as bearers of the priesthood, is to keep the lights on long enough—and bright enough—for as many as possible to see the reckoning coming and choose repentance over ruin. A brotherhood united for something implicitly unites against its opposite; as we cultivate the light of Christ in our lives, we can use it to fight against Satan's dark operation and save more souls.

The Night's Nature

Evil men have operated in the darkness since the Earth's first family. "For, from the days of Cain, there was a secret combination, and their works were in the dark..."[27] Adam's son covenanted with Satan "in secret," becoming "Mahan, the master of this great secret."[28] His posterity continued this lu-

26 D&C 123:12–15.
27 Moses 5:51.
28 Moses 5:29–31.

crative relationship, securing power by doing Satan's bidding. Lamech, for example, "entered into a covenant with Satan, after the manner of Cain, wherein he became Master Mahan, master of that great secret which was administered unto Cain by Satan."[29] It was a tried-and-true recipe that the adversary could cook up in each new generation.

Others of Adam's posterity aimed to shine a light into this darkness. "Irad, the son of Enoch, having known their secret, began to reveal it unto the sons of Adam." For this whistle-blowing effort, he was murdered—not "for the sake of getting gain, but [Lamech] slew him for the oath's sake." Thus did those operating in secret aim to keep it a secret. Yet the word got out, and the records kept by faithful people documented the oaths and covenants and activities of these conspiring actors. These records were "brought across the great deep" by the Jaredite group.[30] In them was "an account concerning them of old, that they by their secret plans did obtain kingdoms and great glory."[31] And this account was descriptive enough such that a new secret combination was formed, patterned off of preceding versions, with murder and the acquisition of power and wealth being the primary focus.

Centuries of conspiratorial conflict led to the ultimate collapse of this society—yet a record survived, inscribed on gold plates that were discovered by Limhi's people,[32] translated and shared by Mosiah,[33] and included among the Nephite re-

29 Moses 5:49.
30 Ether 8:9.
31 Ibid.
32 Mosiah 8:9, 11–12.
33 Mosiah 28:11–19.

cords kept and handed down from one prophetic scribe to another. So sensitive was the situation that Alma taught his son Helaman:

> I command you that ye retain all their oaths, and their covenants, and their agreements in their secret abominations; yea, and all their signs and their wonders ye shall keep from this people, that they know them not, lest peradventure they should fall into darkness also and be destroyed.
>
> Therefore ye shall keep these secret plans of their oaths and their covenants from this people... trust not those secret plans unto this people, but teach them an everlasting hatred against sin and iniquity.[34]

Helaman did his part and retained these records so as to limit the spread of secret combinations. But it wasn't enough to stop the rise of Gadianton and his band of misfits. Mormon explains that "those secret oaths and covenants did not come forth unto Gadianton from the records which were delivered unto Helaman; but behold, they were put into the heart of Gadianton by that same being who did entice our first parents to partake of the forbidden fruit."[35] Satan didn't need dusty records or oral history to preserve his operation. Sure, his followers "hand down their plots, and their oaths, and their covenants, and their plans of awful wickedness, from generation to generation according as he can get hold upon the hearts of

---

34 Alma 37:27, 29, 32; see also Helaman 6:25.
35 Helaman 6:26.

the children of men."[36] But he could also start the cycle anew with anyone interested. Moroni didn't even bother to "write the manner of their oaths and combinations" since God revealed to him that "they are had among all people."[37]

Secrecy, then, is the night's native element—the darkness that we are called to illuminate. Wrong rarely parades in daylight; it thrives by hiding,[38] deceiving,[39] and denying its own existence.[40] It plants in the hearts of men whose designs we cannot easily discern.[41] Satan's mortal minions "seek deep to hide their counsels from the Lord"[42]—and though nothing escapes God's sight, their smokescreens often blind us. Deprived of accurate context, we swallow manufactured narratives and mistake polished lies for truth. Fighting the night of wrong therefore starts with recognizing that much wickedness works offstage, shielded by deception, and that those who drag it into the light often pay in reputation, livelihood, or even life.

The night of wrong is not sustained by threats alone; its real power is persuasion. Picture a man intent on building a secret combination today. He knows fear will get him only so far—people who comply at gunpoint look for the first chance to break free. So instead, he dangles benefits: quick money, insider status, and immunity from consequence. Satan used pre-

36 Helaman 6:30.
37 Ether 8:20.
38 2 Nephi 27:27.
39 D&C 10:25, 50:3, 123:12.
40 2 Nephi 28:22.
41 D&C 38:29, 89:4.
42 2 Nephi 28:9.

cisely that pitch with Cain—"Swear unto me by thy throat"—then sweetened it with the promise, "I will deliver thy brother Abel into thine hands."[43] The lure worked. It worked again centuries later when the workers of darkness "seduced the more part of the righteous until they had come down to believe in their works and partake of their spoils, and to join with them in their secret murders and combinations."[44] Or think of Giddianhi's letter to Lachoneus: "unite with us and become acquainted with our secret works, and become our brethren that ye may be like unto us—not our slaves, but our brethren and partners of all our substance."[45] Evil people in every era employ the same sales line.

The seduction began even earlier—in premortality—when Lucifer assured a third of the hosts of heaven that they could proverbially "eat, drink, and be merry" with guaranteed salvation.[46] That message still resonates through broad cultural boulevards with wide gates that lead to destruction—yet "many there be which go in thereat."[47] The promise is always the same: shortcut joy, shortcut wealth, and shortcut glory. What the tempter never discloses are the crash at the end of the shortcut—since "wickedness never was happiness"[48]—and the iron chains that replace the flaxen cords once the bargain is sealed. Recognizing this pattern is essential for watchmen on the towers: wherever advantage is offered without ac-

43 Moses 5:29, 33.
44 Helaman 6:38.
45 3 Nephi 3:7.
46 2 Nephi 28:7-8.
47 Matthew 7:13.
48 Alma 41:10.

countability, wherever pleasure is sold as consequence-free, the night of wrong is at work, inviting new recruits.

The third primary characteristic of the night of wrong is its slow speed—at least at first. While secret combinations began to spread, the Nephites enjoyed peace and prosperity.[49] Eventually, an "exceeding great pride... had gotten into the hearts of the people" which "did grow upon them from day to day."[50] That incremental seep of vanity—like a steady drip eroding a stone foundation—created invisible fissures long before any outward collapse appeared. Scripture chronicles this measured creep again and again; evil prefers a silent advance to a sudden assault.

Embracing evil is never a flipped switch. It's more like a lingering sunset: light yields by imperceptible degrees until darkness finally feels inevitable. Satan's strategy exploits exactly that pace. He "leadeth them by the neck with a flaxen cord" first soft and scarcely felt, then tight and unbreakable as iron chains.[51] Temptations trace the same path—one curious taste, one casual glance, and one "harmless" wager—each thread spun so fine it seems dismissible, yet together they bind the soul. Most who awaken in bondage arrived there step-by-step.

The night of wrong's initial slowness threatens today just as it shadowed ancient societies. President Gordon B. Hinckley underscored that danger when he introduced "The Family: A Proclamation to the World" in 1995: "With so much of

49 Helaman 3:23–35.
50 Helaman 3:36.
51 2 Nephi 26:22, 28:19.

sophistry that is passed off as truth, with so much of deception concerning standards and values, with so much of allurement and enticement to take on the slow stain of the world, we have felt to warn and forewarn."[52] Precisely because the stain advances by degrees, it blends into its surroundings and poses as normal life; almost no one resists what appears harmless.

Many Latter-day Saints, intent on safeguarding their own households, overlook the moral dry rot eating away at the culture that influences those very homes. Reassured that "all is well in Zion,"[53] they permit shades of evil until the accumulated grime feels ordinary. In tolerating each tiny compromise, they exchange the power to purify society for the ease of fitting in—seduced to partake in the plentiful spoils offered. If we fail to understand the night of wrong's nature, then the day of brotherhood will never be realized. We cannot rise above a problem we don't even perceive.

The Night of Slumber

In a modern parable revealed to Joseph Smith about the importance of vigilance, the Lord emphasized how critical it is to be on guard against the night of wrong. The lord of a vineyard instructed his servants to plant twelve olive trees and "set watchmen round about them, and build a tower, that one may overlook the land round about."[54] The servants com-

52 Gordon B. Hinckley, "Stand Strong against the Wiles of the World," *Ensign*, November 1995, https://churchofjesuschrist.org/study/general-conference/1995/10/stand-strong-against-the-wiles-of-the-world.

53 2 Nephi 28:21.

54 D&C 101:45.

plied initially, planting the trees and appointing watchmen—but as they began to build the tower, disputes arose among them. Some questioned, "What need hath [our] lord of this tower, seeing this is a time of peace?"[55] These now-slothful servants who failed to comply and prepare for the enemy's advances now found themselves overcome: "The enemy came by night, and broke down the hedge; and the servants of the nobleman arose and were affrighted, and fled; and the enemy destroyed their works, and broke down the olive trees."[56] The lord's response was predictable:

> Ought ye not to have done even as I commanded you, and—after ye had planted the vineyard, and built the hedge round about, and set watchmen upon the walls thereof—built the tower also, and set a watchman upon the tower, and watched for my vineyard, and not have fallen asleep, lest the enemy should come upon you?
>
> And behold, the watchman upon the tower would have seen the enemy while he was yet afar off; and then ye could have made ready and kept the enemy from breaking down the hedge thereof, and saved my vineyard from the hands of the destroyer.[57]

Interestingly, the servants' failure to build a tower and have a watchman stand guard is equated in the parable to falling asleep. This brings additional context to President Benson's observation that the priesthood has been reduced to "sleep-

55 D&C 101:48.
56 D&C 101:51.
57 D&C 101:53–54.

ing giants"; slumber is inaction. The call throughout scripture to awake—"awake, put on strength";[58] "awake... and shake off the awful chains by which ye are bound";[59] "awake to a sense of your awful situation"[60]—is therefore a call to act. The condemnation early Latter-day Saints brought upon themselves for their own inaction—a consequence that has not been resolved—contains the same requirement. Saints would have to "not only... say, but to *do* according to that which I have written—that they may bring forth fruit meet for their Father's kingdom."[61] The servants in the parable never renounced their master; they just stalled, debated, and deferred until opportunity was gone and the enemy was inside the gates. They failed to act and were correspondingly condemned.

This parable speaks precisely to us, for we similarly slumber during the night of wrong—we fail to fight back and shine a light. God wants nefarious deeds "made manifest in the light,"[62] yet too many Latter-day Saints confine their light to shine only within the walls of their home, letting evil spread throughout our communities unchecked. The night of wrong banks on this kind of spiritual drowsiness. Satan does not necessarily need us wicked; he only needs us busy, distracted, and convinced that vigilance can wait for a crisis. But towers cannot be thrown up overnight, and watchmen serve little purpose if the enemy has already deeply infiltrated the vineyard.

---

58 Isaiah 51:9.
59 2 Nephi 1:13.
60 Ether 8:24.
61 D&C 84:57–58; emphasis added.
62 2 Nephi 30:17.

In addition to falling asleep, the parable describes these servants as being "very slothful," for they "hearkened not unto the commandments of their lord."[63] This offers another lesson regarding how we ought to act with respect to the night of wrong. The Lord wants us to be proactive, not reactive—He wants us to prepare ahead for the enemy, not wait until the threat is imminent. He commands us to act so we are not acted upon.[64] And He wants us to avoid this sloth by using our agency to heed His commandments to watch for and reject evil:

> For behold, it is not meet that I should command in all things; for he that is compelled in all things, the same is a slothful and not a wise servant; wherefore he receiveth no reward. Verily I say, men should be anxiously engaged in a good cause, and do many things of their own free will, and bring to pass much righteousness;
>
> For the power is in them, wherein they are agents unto themselves. And inasmuch as men do good they shall in nowise lose their reward. But he that doeth not anything until he is commanded, and receiveth a commandment with doubtful heart, and keepeth it with slothfulness, the same is damned.[65]

The day of brotherhood will dawn only when the men who hold the priesthood trade sleep for sentry duty, finish the towers assigned to them, and keep watch to ensure the night of wrong does not spread. Satan hates the light. We must bring

63 D&C 101:50.
64 2 Nephi 2:26.
65 D&C 58:26–29.

it. He prefers us asleep—inactive. We must rise up above this paralyzing slumber and be light-bearers to expose the enemy.

Today's Night

The scriptures offer us examples of how past nights of wrong looked—with vanity, pride, and secret combinations spreading throughout societies we only know a little about. And despite knowing that we ought to "liken all scriptures unto us, that it might be for our profit and learning,"[66] we often struggle to pair parables and prophetic teachings to our busy, modern lives. So if we are to thwart the advance of the night of wrong—if we as the day of brotherhood are to unite against evil and spread God's light—what does this look like in our day? Let's revisit the three traits previously mentioned and then expand upon each to consider how these traits manifest in our modern society.

Secrecy

The paranoia that pervades the post-9/11 world led, among other things, to the development of new surveillance programs by the National Security Agency (NSA) under the guise that rooting out terrorism required mass monitoring of communications in order to stop a future attack. This global panopticon, of course, was built in secret—and as whispers circulated regarding its existence, top officials outright denied it. In March 2013, then-Director of National Intelligence

66 1 Nephi 19:23.

James Clapper testified to Congress about the NSA's activities. One senator asked him, "Does the NSA collect any type of data at all on millions or hundreds of millions of Americans?" Clapper responded, "No, sir... Not wittingly."[67] This was a blatant lie. Not only was the NSA collecting data on millions of Americans, but it was also doing so intentionally and systematically.

This televised interview was a transparent deception known by those with proper security clearances and involvement in the NSA's programs—including Edward Snowden, whose involvement pricked his conscience and compelled him to leak thousands of documents detailing the NSA's extensive surveillance programs of innocent people. Snowden's whistleblowing actions were widely condemned by government officials who wanted to maintain the secrecy of their unconstitutional surveillance. As former Representative Ron Paul often said, "Truth is treason in an empire of lies." Snowden, who aimed to defend the Constitution and the rights of innocent people, was forced to flee the country to evade capture by the intelligence agencies whose secret works he had exposed. In the shadowy corridors of power, secrecy often serves as the first line of defense for those who perpetrate evil.

Another act of illumination into those shadowy corridors was met with similar reprisal. Julian Assange, the founder of WikiLeaks, exposed classified documents related to the wars

67 "The NSA's Word Games Explained: How the Government Deceived Congress in the Debate over Surveillance Powers," Electronic Frontier Foundation, June 11, 2013, https://www.eff.org/deeplinks/2013/06/director-national-intelligences-word-games-explained-how-government-deceived.

in Iraq and Afghanistan, bringing to light war crimes and unethical practices that had been deliberately hidden from public scrutiny. This data dump included, among other revelations: footage showing a US Apache helicopter attack in Baghdad that killed multiple civilians, including two Reuters journalists;[68] unlawful killings of civilians, including the notorious Nisour Square massacre in Baghdad, where nearly twenty civilians were killed;[69] systematic torture and abuse of detainees, including electric shocks, water torture, and mock executions;[70] and much more.

For this act of truth-telling, Assange was charged with eighteen offenses, including conspiracy to commit computer intrusion and violations of the Espionage Act, carrying a possible sentence of up to 175 years in prison if convicted.[71] After fourteen years of legal battles and imprisonment, he was released in June 2024 after a plea deal. But his actions were perceived as so treacherous to those in power that senior CIA officials apparently plotted to kidnap and kill Assange, "going so far as to request 'sketches' or 'options' for how to assassi-

---

68 "Collateral Murder" *The New York Times*, January 24, 2011, https://www.nytimes.com/video/multimedia/1248069533084/collateral-murder.html.

69 "From Errand to Fatal Shot to Hail of Fire to 17 Deaths," *The New York Times*, October 3, 2007, https://www.nytimes.com/2007/10/03/world/middleeast/03firefight.html.

70 "https://www.nytimes.com/video/multimedia/1248069533084/collateral-murder.html," *The Guardian*, October 22, 2010, https://www.theguardian.com/world/2010/oct/22/iraq-war-logs-military-leaks.

71 "Julian Assange's mission was to change the world - but at what cost?," CNN, June 25, 2024, https://www.cnn.com/2024/04/27/europe/julian-assange-profile-intl-cmd/index.html.

nate him."[72] Former Secretary of State Hillary Clinton allegedly asked if the WikiLeaks founder could be killed in a drone strike.[73] Those who unveil dark deeds are a target for elimination by those who hate the light.

More alarmingly, but unsurprisingly given how secret combinations act—ruled by the laws of their wickedness, which includes shielding fellow evildoers from legal accountability—no one has ever been held responsible for these war crimes. There have been no arrests. Nobody was even fired. And yet a publisher who exposed these crimes was relentlessly persecuted for revealing secret documents showing unlawful and immoral activity.

These modern episodes—a tiny sampling from a lengthy list of examples of governement corruption and secret evildoing from around the world and throughout history—echo the ancient pattern: when wrongdoing is hidden by those who wield and aspire for power, anyone who drags it into the open is considered a threat. Mass surveillance carried out without warrants, battlefield atrocities shielded under layers of secrecy, and the ruthless pursuit of those who publicize them, all prove that the night of wrong still depends on darkness for survival. Until light reaches these shadowed corners, the destroyer remains inside the hedge and the vineyard stays at risk.

---

72 "Kidnapping, assassination and a London shoot-out: Inside the CIA's secret war plans against WikiLeaks," Yahoo News, September 26, 2021, https://www.yahoo.com/news/kidnapping-assassination-and-a-london-shoot-out-inside-the-ci-as-secret-war-plans-against-wiki-leaks-090057786.html.

73 "Clinton: I don't recall joking about droning Julian Assange," Politico, October 4, 2016, https://www.politico.com/story/2016/10/hillary-clinton-julian-assange-229123.

Seduction

Seduction is the night's marketing department—its recruiting engine to funnel people into its ranks. Some lures appeal directly to the appetite: the instant dopamine of pornography, stimulants, or simply doomscrolling social media. At first glance, these seem purely personal choices, yet they are "flaxen cords" that soon harden into chains, turning users from actors into objects acted upon.[74] But the adversary's more sophisticated tactic is to link pleasure with patronage: he invites us to support secret combinations in exchange for a cut of the spoils.[75] It's one thing to misallocate our time and energy in pursuit of seductive personal pleasures; it's another to be enticed to allocate our time and energy to support—wittingly or otherwise—the organized efforts of Satan's mortal minions.

The political version of this is familiar to most. Candidates aspiring for power promise all kinds of perks—debt forgiveness, new programs, expanded entitlements, industry subsidies, economic stimuli, and more. These are the promised spoils of secret combinations, used to seduce support and affiliation. The horse trade couldn't be more clear: give me power, and I'll provide these benefits to you. Voters so seduced scarcely question the misdeeds of those for whom they voted, whether undeclared wars that vaporize innocents with drone strikes or the ballooning debt that will shackle their grandchildren. The moral cost is outsourced to distant battlefields

74 2 Nephi 2:26.
75 Helaman 6:38.

and future generations, while self-interested voters enjoy the short-term gain.

Let's consider two examples of how deep this seduction goes, and how significantly it compromises the morality of those affected. First, abortion. A hookup culture where casual sex is normalized depends on the illusion that consequences can be avoided (or, aborted). Legalized, on-demand abortion supplies the kill switch: fornicate freely and, if life begins, terminate it under cover of law. The arrangement enriches clinics, props up pharmaceutical corporations, and fuels political machines, while seducing participants to believe that there is such a thing as consequence-free sexual intimacy. Lucifer's premortal sales pitch—"sin and still be saved"—echoes in every promise that personal pleasure can be divorced from eternal law. Abortion is thus not merely a medical procedure or a political talking point; it is the flagship sacrament of a modern death cult that trades helpless life for momentary ease. When a society can be seduced into sanctioning the destruction of life into law, the night of wrong has done its work—sanctifying bloodshed and drafting ordinary people into complicity with darkness.

For the children fortunate enough to escape the fate of some 73 million children aborted each year,[76] the vast majority are enrolled by their parents into Caesar's indoctrination camps—state schools funded through coercive taxation using

---

76 "Despite Bans, Number of Abortions in the United States Increased in 2023," Guttmacher Institute, march 2024, https://www.guttmacher.org/2024/03/despite-bans-number-abortions-united-states-increased-2023.

curriculum controlled by the government and produced to favor its objectives. Parents outsource their primary responsibility—the care and education of their children during their most intellectually and spiritually formative years of development—to an institution that promises academic excellence but actually produces intellectual mediocrity and spiritual alienation. What is actually provided—and actually what parents prize the most—is day care, relieving parents of the obligation to educate, entertain, and be around their children during the day. But this perk comes with a price, and the degree to which this schooling system has alienated its attendees from God is proof of how seduced parents have become into compliantly surrendering their children's spiritual health in exchange for short-term parental relief. Remember what Voddie Baucham said: we "cannot continue to send our children to Caesar for their education and be surprised when they come home as Romans."[77] Mic drop.

Whatever the perk being promised, the pattern is the same: offer immediate gratification, hide the real cost, and enlist the consumer as a silent partner in darkness. These offers are abundant and everywhere in our highly interconnected society. On-demand entertainment, pornography, fast food, propaganda, pharmaceuticals, and more bombard us with attempts to get something now for which the expense won't come due until later, if at all. These seductions gratify the appetite and conceal the invoice. A culture trained to chase sec-

77 Voddie Baucham Jr., *Family Driven Faith: Doing What It Takes to Raise Sons and Daughters Who Walk with God* (Wheaton: Crossway, 2007), 202.

onds of dopamine is quietly mortgaging its future—physical health, financial freedom, and spiritual clarity—all for a hit that fades by nightfall. Those who would carry light into this night must begin by refusing to support it. We cannot expose secret wrongs with one hand while subsidizing them with the other.

Slowness

The drift into darkness is seldom a flashy headline; it is rather the quiet, years-long slide of norms once taken for granted. Marriage is a prime example. When "The Family: A Proclamation to the World" was shared in 1995, it was met with what can best be described as a collective shrug. "Marriage between man and woman is essential to His eternal plan,"[78] it said. Yet even then the institution was already eroding. Married-couple households comprised 47 percent of all households in the United States in 2022, down from 71 percent in 1970.[79] Since 1900, the US marriage rate has declined 54 percent, peaking in 1920 at a rate that is almost triple today's rate.[80] In 1980, six percent of forty-year-olds in the US had never married; today that number exceeds 25

78 Hinckley, "Stand Strong against the Wiles of the World."

79 "Census Bureau Releases New Estimates on Families and Living Arrangements," United States Census Bureau, May 30, 2024, https://www.census.gov/newsroom/press-releases/2024/families-living-arrangements.html.

80 "Marriage: More than a Century of Change, 1900-2022," Bowling Green State University, accessed February 9, 2025, https://www.bgsu.edu/ncfmr/resources/data/family-profiles/FP-24-10.html.

percent.[81] One demographic projection suggests that a third of young adults will not marry by age forty-five and maybe never marry.[82] A social relationship deemed "essential" to God's plan is increasingly considered nonessential by many of His children. Fertility has followed the same downward slope: the rate today is at a historic low, with 1.62 children per woman in 2023.[83] Global fertility has halved since 1950 while the number of women in the reproductive age bracket has tripled.[84] What began as slight postponements of marriage or childbearing has become a structural shift in which careers and leisure routinely outrank covenant and children.

Sexual identity illustrates the same incremental cultural takeover. In 1995, nearly nobody disputed that human beings were "male and female," as the Proclamation affirmed, or that "gender is an essential characteristic" of one's identity that is not fluid or simply "assigned" at birth. Yet today, nearly 20 percent of Gen Z identifies as lesbian, gay, bisexual, or transgender.[85] This shift in sexual identity has affected so-

---

81 "A record-high share of 40-year-olds in the U.S. have never been married," Pew Research Center, June 28, 2023, https://www.pewresearch.org/short-reads/2023/06/28/a-record-high-share-of-40-year-olds-in-the-us-have-never-been-married/.

82 "The closing of the American heart," *Deseret News*, April 30, 2024, https://www.deseret.com/family/2024/04/30/marriage-benefits-for-adults/.

83 "Births: Provisional Data for 2023," National Center for Health Statistics, accessed February 11, 2025, https://www.cdc.gov/nchs/data/vsrr/vsrr035.pdf.

84 "The Problem with 'Too Few,'" United Nations Population Fund, accessed February 11, 2025, https://www.unfpa.org/swp2023/too-few.

85 "7.2 Percent of U.S. Adults Identify as LGBT," Statista, February 28, 2023, https://www.statista.com/chart/18228/share-of-

ciety at large, including Latter-day Saints; only 78 percent of 18 to 25-year-old Saints say they are straight.[86] A second study confirmed the data, finding that about one in five Millennial or Gen Z Latter-day Saints identifies as LGBT.[87] Social contagion, peer applause, and media saturation have shifted boundaries slowly enough that many scarcely noticed the line move until objective truths about sex and gender were recast as bigotry.

Of course, the slow onset of darkness is not confined only to issues found in the Proclamation. Consider, as a final example, the topic of war. Where Latter-day Saints were once commanded to "renounce war and proclaim peace,"[88] they now largely do the reverse. Years into the Iraq War, for example, Gallup pollsters found that out of all major religious groups, "Mormons are the most likely to favor" the war.[89] An astounding 72 percent of American Latter-day Saints supported sending troops to Iraq to fight a war that had no justifiable basis.[90] One sees in this a more recent example of what Spencer W. Kimball wrote about in 1976, calling the Saints a

---

americans-identifying-as-lgbt/.

86 Ryan Burge, "Gender, Sexual Orientation and Religion Among American College Students," Graphs About Religion, September 18, 2023, https://www.graphsaboutreligion.com/p/gender-sexual-orientation-and-religion.

87 "Rising numbers of young adult Mormons in the US are gay, lesbian or bisexual," Religion News, June 21, 2021, https://religionnews.com/2021/06/21/rising-number-of-adult-mormons-in-the-us-are-gay-lesbian-or-bisexual/.

88 D&C 98:16.

89 "Among Religious Groups, Jewish Americans Most Strongly Oppose War," Gallup, February 23, 2007, https://news.gallup.com/poll/26677/among-religious-groups-jewish-americans-most-strongly-oppose-war.aspx.

90 Among other reasons, the war was not justified based on the criteria in D&C 98.

"warlike people" easily distracted from following God. Recall his words: "When enemies rise up, we commit vast resources to the fabrication of gods of stone and steel—ships, planes, missiles, fortifications—and depend on them for protection and deliverance. When threatened, we become anti-enemy instead of pro-kingdom of God."[91]

Few Saints intentionally trade prophetic counsel for partisan talking points. Rather, the slide into supporting Caesar's fleshy arm begins with small concessions: a shrug when civilian casualties are dismissed by those in power as "collateral damage"; a rationalization that "strong defense" always outweighs Isaiah's call to "beat swords into plowshares"; an uncritical cheer when more military spending results in employment for one's friends and family; or satiating a lustful desire to seek vengeance in response to a perceived harm by the enemy. Each accommodation feels reasonable, even patriotic, yet each one nudges hearts a degree further toward the arm of flesh. Over a generation those tiny turns have added up to a wholesale inversion of priorities—anti-enemy first, pro-kingdom of God second. Just as marriage eroded through normalized cohabitation and postponed vows, and gender norms blurred through unchallenged slogans and celebrity appeal, devotion to peace has withered through a steady stream of votes of confidence in Caesar's steel. Slow drift is still drift, and if uncorrected, it carries Zion's people downstream into the very night they were commanded to dispel. The greatest

91 Spencer W. Kimball, "The False Gods We Worship," *Ensign*, June 1976, 3.

victories of darkness are won not by sudden conquest, but by steady surrender—one overlooked inch at a time.

To Waste and to Wear Out

In one sense, the successful spread of darkness is inevitable. Scriptures foretell of a latter-day apocalypse—a society so spiritually decayed that "darkness covereth the earth, and gross darkness the minds of the people."[92] The Lord reveals his response: vengeance that includes "a day of wrath, a day of burning, a day of desolation, of weeping, of mourning, and of lamentation."[93] The Spirit showed Nephi a vision of our day with corrupt churches, pride, and secret combinations.[94] Mormon similarly prophesied of "a day when there shall be great pollutions upon the face of the earth; there shall be murders, and robbing, and lying, and deceivings, and whoredoms, and all manner of abominations."[95] That day—better put, that night of wrong—includes "your churches, yea, even every one, [which] have become polluted because of the pride of your hearts."[96] It's not a pretty picture, and a cursory review of these and similar scriptures[97] might lead one to become

---

92 D&C 112:23.

93 D&C 112:24; note that in the following two verses, God says that such vengeance will begin first upon his house—we Latter-day Saints—who have falsely professed to know Him.

94 2 Nephi 28:3–14, 20–23.

95 Mormon 8:31.

96 Mormon 8:36.

97 Matthew 24:7; 1 Nephi 14:17; 2 Nephi 30:10; D&C 34:9; D&C 45:26, 31–33; Moses 7:60–61. Oh, and pretty much the entire book of Revelation.

fatalistic about the future. After all, if darkness is prophesied to be so pervasive, what hope have we?

Yet, amid this prophesied gloom, hope endures—not through grand revolutions or miraculous interventions alone, but through the quiet power of individual agency, a divine gift that even the darkest regimes cannot fully extinguish. Consider the life of Aleksandr Solzhenitsyn, a man who dwelt in the heart of twentieth-century tyranny under the Soviet Union, a system that mirrored the "gross darkness" of our latter days with its web of deception, oppression, and spiritual decay.[98] Imprisoned in the brutal Gulag labor camps for criticizing Stalin in a private letter, Solzhenitsyn endured years of suffering, witnessing the murder of millions, a web of lies, and the systematic crushing of human dignity. He had every reason to succumb to despair, to become fatalistic about the inexorable advance of evil. Released from the Gulag years later, he chose instead to spread light into the darkness by secretly authoring *The Gulag Archipelago*, a monumental exposé of the Soviet camp system's atrocities, which was smuggled to the West and published in 1973, igniting global outrage; the furious Soviet authorities responded by branding him a traitor, leading directly to his arrest and forced exile in February 1974.

On the eve of that arrest, he penned a defiant essay titled "Live Not by Lies," calling his fellow citizens to a simple yet profound act of resistance: refuse to participate in the falsehoods that sustain the darkness.[99] Solzhenitsyn understood

98 See Joseph Pearce, *Solzhenitsyn: A Soul in Exile* (Ignatius Press, 2011).

99 "Live Not By Lies," The Aleksandr Solzhenitsyn Center, ac-

that totalitarian evil thrives not merely on violence but on the complicity of ordinary people who, out of fear or convenience, lend their voices and actions to its lies. "Violence has nothing to cover itself with but lies," he wrote, "and lies can only persist through violence."[100] In the Soviet regime, citizens were pressured to applaud sham elections, teach distorted history, and echo propaganda that exalted the state while concealing its atrocities—all to preserve meager comforts like employment or safety for their families. To go along was to become, in essence, a host for the parasitic forces of darkness, allowing evil to feed on one's soul and propagate through society. But Solzhenitsyn insisted that individuals held the key to liberation: "...a personal nonparticipation in lies! Even if all is covered by lies, even if all is under their rule, let us resist in the smallest way: Let their rule hold not through me!"[101] By choosing truth in daily acts—refusing to sign false documents, attend coerced rallies, or utter insincere praises—one could starve the beast, reclaim spiritual independence, and hasten the system's defeat.

Even if society is decaying in the aggregate, we need not be tainted too. Indeed, we are called by God to live not by lies—to be truth tellers in a world full of deception.[102] "I sent you out to testify and warn the people," He said, "and it becometh

---

cessed July 17, 2025, https://www.solzhenitsyncenter.org/live-not-by-lies.

100 Ibid.

101 Ibid.

102 D&C 50:2–3. See also Ephesians 4:14; Revelation 12:9; James 1:22; D&C 52:14; Moses 4:4.

every man who hath been warned to warn his neighbor."[103] He has prepared tools to "shine forth in darkness... that I may discover unto [us] the works of [our] brethren, yea their secret works, their works of darkness."[104] He "will bring forth out of darkness unto light all their secret works and their abominations."[105] We—the brotherhood, Christ's disciples—are to be the instrument in His hands to do so. And this is how we remove the condemnation that hangs over us—by not only talking about but actually *doing* what God has required of us.[106] We must offer worthy fruit from our labor and stop the "slow stain of the world." We must awaken. We must rise up.

But how? What does it actually look like, in our modern day, to be a light-bearer into the darkness? The opportunities are as varied as the evils they can expose. Each is first predicated on the assumption that we possess light—that we recognize deception and can identify the masked evil that has deceived so many others. From there, combating the night of wrong might look like any of the following:

- Seek transparency. Master your state's open-records laws and file public-records requests for budgets, contracts, emails, and text messages that may reveal corruption. Summarize the findings in plain language, post source documents online, and share them with trustworthy reporters or citizen journalists who can amplify the story.

103 D&C 88:81.
104 Alma 37:23.
105 Alma 37:25.
106 D&C 84:57.

- Rally others to your cause. Establish a nonprofit watchdog group with a diverse board—lawyers, accountants, data analysts, and communicators. Pooling skills and donations gives you staying power, credibility with media outlets, and leverage with officials who might ignore a lone critic.
- Produce investigative media. Give truth a microphone. Launch a podcast or video channel, write on Substack, or craft a short documentary that exposes a specific evil. Tell compelling stories, cite primary documents, and package complex facts so ordinary viewers stay engaged. Evil people have long been producing propaganda to further their aims. It's high time we do the same—propagating true ideas and exposing deceptions.
- Organize people to learn more. Host town-hall forums or livestream panels featuring topic experts and whistle-blowers. Record and distribute the event so the audience multiplies beyond the room. Always end with a clear call to action—links, petitions, service opportunities—so curiosity can turn into commitment.
- Lead a boycott campaign. Identify companies bankrolling things like abortion, war profiteering, porn distribution, or food adulteration, and document the evidence with sources. Publish clear, shareable lists that highlight both the offenders and ethical alternatives. Urge consumers to reroute their dollars, then track the results: lost contracts, falling share prices, or pub-

lic pivots that prove money talks. Pitch the story to local and national media, use social platforms to amplify wins, and make sure the targeted corporation feels the financial sting—and knows exactly why it hurts.

- Coordinate peaceful protests or prayer vigils. Gather outside abortion clinics, capitol buildings, corporate headquarters, or unjust court hearings to bear nonviolent witness. Maintain a reverent tone, comply with local laws, and pair the vigil with literature or QR codes that explain the issue you're confronting, and offer practical help to victims and concerned citizens.
- Sponsor public debates. Invite articulate voices from both sides of hot-button topics—gender policy, endless wars, corporate subsidies, etc.—under neutral, respectful moderation. Record and share the debate to model that light embraces scrutiny and that truth emerges stronger when ideas meet open examination.

These are but a few of many such examples and are meant to help you ponder what action looks like within your sphere of influence. Recall in the parable of the talents that the servant who used his talents to pursue and obtain more was considered "good and faithful," whereas another was called "wicked and slothful" for failing to do the same.[107] That servant admitted he was "afraid" and consequently had his talent taken from him.[108] Here's the Lord's counsel: "For unto every

107 Matthew 25:21, 26.
108 Matthew 25:25–28..

one that hath shall be given, and he shall have abundance: but from him that hath not shall be taken away even that which he hath."[109] What talents has God blessed you with that should be developed so that you help "shine forth in darkness"?

Joseph's charge to document corruption and expose evil deeds echoes across the centuries: it is not optional work for a few activists—it is an "imperative duty" resting on every Latter-day Saint—particularly those who are part of the priesthood. To "waste and wear out our lives" in bringing hidden wrongs to light is simply an outward expression of loving God and our neighbor in an age of organized deception. The prophecies of deepening darkness are not permission to retreat; they are a summons to stand watch, document truth, and warn the weary—even at personal cost. When men of God rise to that commission, the night of wrong loses its shadowy cover, the honest find courage, and the Lord's promised arm of deliverance moves in full view of a world that can no longer claim it did not know.

---

109 Matthew 25:29.

THE CHURCH WAITS

In the LDS hymnal, the entire third verse of Merrill's lyrics was expunged. Priesthood holders who, from their youth, have sung or heard his words do not realize that the familiar lyrics are incomplete. It was a surprise to me once I learned about the omission. "Rise up, O men of God!" it reads. "The church for you doth wait, her strength unequal to her task; rise up, and make her great!" We can only speculate as to why this entire section was removed—so speculate we shall. In doing so, we'll continue to rely on Merrill's words as a guide for our actions as men of God and members of The Church of Jesus Christ of Latter-day Saints.

Let's break the verse down into pieces. First, Merrill states that the Church waits for us. What might this mean? The restored Church is intentionally built as a lay kingdom; almost everything it accomplishes depends on ordinary disciples stepping forward. Programs exist—quorums, auxiliaries, and stakes—but they are skeletal frameworks until members supply muscle and movement. The Church is not some independent entity acting of its own accord; the Church is us. Its mission hinges on members rising up to move it forward. Its success is realized only by the independent actions of those who comprise it. God's commandments are realized by independent individuals each taking initiative—not some Borg collective all acting in concert. The Church's mission—to spread the gospel and convert souls—is at the mercy of those who put in the work to make it real. But consider another variation of this statement where we divide Church administration (general authorities, employees, and those involved full time in managing its affairs) from lay Church members. In this context, it is interesting to consider what it might mean for the Church to wait for us. That is, the institutional Church—and those who are employed in its work—waits for us, men of God, to rise up and do *our* work. Taken this way, one might argue that despite all its resources and relationships, there are certain things—including ending the night of wrong—that the institutional Church relies on individual members to do. We'll explore some ideas here in a moment.

The next piece of the verse mentions the Church's strength being unequal to her task. Despite billions in the bank and a membership roster in the millions, the institution is inadequate to discharge the divine duties associated with the Lord's "marvelous work" in these latter days.[1] The reasons should be plainly obvious: a handful of general authorities cannot shepherd billions—local disciples must carry the load; culture change doesn't come by producing new handbooks and holding fifth Sunday lessons—it comes from the aggregated effort of each of us righteously influencing our networks of family and friends; doubling or even tripling the number of full-time missionaries will always pale in comparison to the impact made by members using their agency to proactively

1 D&C 4:1.

preach the gospel to the people they know and care about; global crises surpass the capacity of the Church's humanitarian aid, demonstrating the need for individuals to rise up and respond; and occasional conference talks from inspired leaders will never be enough to counteract the daily bombardment of worldly messages to which we're subjected. Put simply, the institutional Church isn't strong enough to build Zion. Celestial unity won't be engineered in Salt Lake; it grows only when individual hearts and minds are applied to the effort, each adding their own strength. That disparity is by design, not defect. God organized His Church to function more like a body than a factory: the head gives direction, but progress depends on every limb responding.[2] Recognizing this intentional shortfall should cure us of spectator syndrome. The Church's task list—preach the gospel, redeem the dead, perfect the Saints, and care for the poor—has always exceeded its institutional horsepower because the Lord intends the extra capacity to come from consecrated individuals acting under the Spirit's direction. Heaven's timetable for Zion moves at the pace of our personal devotion.

The final piece calls on us to rise up and make the Church great. Taken at surface level, this seems to suggest a focus on improving the image and function of the Church—making it better by lending our energy and efforts to its cause. While true, this word choice hints at a potential deeper meaning, one where *great* has more spiritual substance. Recall that the coming of the Lord is also called great—"the great and last

---

2 1 Corinthians 12:14–21.

day,"[3] or "even that great day when the earth shall be rolled together as a scroll."[4] The Lord says that "it shall be a great day at the time of my coming, for all nations shall tremble."[5] The scriptures offer other instances where this word applies—God's work among the children of men is called great,[6] and Christ says that those who desire greatness should serve others.[7] Webster's 1828 dictionary offers a few relevant definitions for greatness: large in bulk or dimensions; large in number; a large, extensive or unusual degree of any thing; or important and weighty.[8] Sure, by lending our strength, we can enhance the size and scope of the institutional Church. We can minister more, pay tithes and offerings, render service, fulfill callings, and support the missionaries. But the greatness imagined here is, I think, even greater—making the body of Christ more influential, more impactful, and more effective. By rising up to fulfill our heavenly charge, we become great, not simply in terms of quarterly statistics but also in terms of the combined radiance of consecrated lives. Rising up to make the Church great is to supply the very strength God intends for us to use up in His service—strength of courage, conviction, skill, and daily consecration. When that strength is freely offered and focused, the Church ceases to wait and begins to stride; her once-unequal task becomes achievable,

3 Helaman 12:25.
4 Mormon 9:2.
5 D&C 34:8.
6 1 Nephi 14:7.
7 Matthew 20:26.
8 "Great," American Dictionary of the English Language, accessed July 28, 2025, https://webstersdictionary1828.com/Dictionary/great.

and her influence swells until, in the hymn's altered words, she truly moves "in one united throng."

Individual vs. Institutional Effort

The Church is both an institution and a collective of individuals. It has a charge; we individuals are called to support it in advancing those goals. And while it may seem—in times of peace and plenty at least—that the institution and the individuals who compose it have no reason for conflict, there are occasions when the contrast between the institution's mandate and our own becomes apparent. Such times of divine disparity can shake one's faith, primarily if one continues to believe that each individual's actions must always be consistent with and subordinated to those of the Church. But this is not so; there are times where individuals may be called upon by God to do something that the Church is unable or not supposed to do. Let's consider one example.

Getting started in Germany was tough going for the nascent Church. Its first missionary president for the German states arrived in Hamburg on April 3, 1852. Daniel Carn, a German immigrant who had converted to Mormonism in the United States, quickly found disfavor among political leaders and law enforcement. Eight times he was hauled before police and the Hamburg Senate; because he refused to leave, he was thrown in jail. His experience was shared by many of the missionaries—themselves German immigrants who returned to their native land to preach the gospel. John Beck was jailed three times in his hometown of Stuttgart; Ernst Mueller went to jail eleven times in three months. The replacement mission president, George Reiser, was given a two-week prison sentence for "being dangerous to our government."[9] Another mission president, Hugh J. Cannon, tried to calm fears by telling Berlin police of "the church's belief in subjugation to local police," noting "that the well-being of the Imperial Government was the object of their daily prayers."[10] Platitudes didn't placate the Germans; police continued breaking up Sunday services, detaining missionaries, and expelling them under threat of jail.[11]

And yet things calmed down enough over the decades enough for a network of local congregations to flourish throughout Germany, composed of individuals who chose not to emigrate to the American Zion. By 1925, there were over 11,000 members of the Church in Germany—a testament to the tenacity of missionaries over the previous several decades. That year, though, a baby boy was born whose actions would soon highlight the fragility of the Church's institutional relations and its willingness to accommodate individuals whose decisions conflicted with its own. It was Helmuth Hübener.

While young Helmuth was approaching the age of baptism, his country was quickly being overtaken by the National Socialist German Workers' Party, or Nazis. Adolf Hitler had been appointed chancellor on January 30, 1933; following the Reichstag Fire and the passage of the Enabling Act, which

---

9 David Conley Nelson, *Moroni and the Swastika* (Norman, University of Oklahoma Press, 2015), 28.

10 Ibid., 38.

11 Ibid., 39.

gave Hitler dictatorial powers. On July 14, the Nazi Party was declared the only legal political party in the country. That September, a Gestapo agent came knocking on the door of the mission headquarters in central Berlin. Oliver Budget, the mission president, fielded some questions and reassured the officer that Mormons were submissive to the state. He doubled down on his remarks in a written letter to the Gestapo the following day, in which he elaborated on: the pronatalist policies of the Church, resemblant of such policies by the Nazis, with the expectation that every member multiply and replenish the earth; the self-reliance of American missionaries and economic benefit to the German economy; his personal pride in the German culture and history as a missionary decades prior; and, most critically, the Church's neutrality in policies. Budge wrote:

> [Mormons] are taught, especially, to be able to class themselves with the best citizens of the country, and to support, in the full sense of the word, the ordinances and laws of the town, the state, and the country in which they live. The authorities of our Church have no advice to give regarding party politics... we teach that the present party in power, and the laws governing the country, be supported by the members of the church.[12]

Budge's efforts were but a small sample of the interactions between Church officials and Nazi party leaders, demonstrating the earnestness of the desire on the part of Mormon lead-

12 Ibid., 94–95.

ers to make friends with German rulers to ensure the safety of Church members and the ability of the Church's missionary work to continue. The price was deemed worth it by leaders who—some reluctantly, and many cheerfully—modified church curriculum to remove any reference to Jews or Israel, including Sunday School lessons, hymns, and other material;[13] included Nazi insignia, such as flags, and Hitler's portrait, in Church meetings;[14] played Hitler's speeches during or after Church meetings, compelling congregants to listen;[15] enthusiastically and reflexively repeated the "Heil Hitler" salute;[16] expelled Jews from church services;[17] denied legal assistance to Mormon Jews wishing to emigrate to America to escape the Hitler regime prior to the war;[18] published op-eds and other material affirming that Nazis and Mormons shared several overlapping interests, and emphasized that one could be a good Mormon and a good citizen of the Nazi state;[19] and on and on.

This institutional appeasement was challenged by the individual actions of young Helmuth, who, as a teenager, chose a very different path—one of secret confrontation. Initially an enthusiastic member of the Hitler Youth,[20] the Latter-day Saint teen became quickly disillusioned as he read widely from books, including those the Nazis had banned, and listened to

---

13 Ibid., 98, 103–104.
14 Ibid., 11, 293.
15 Ibid., 6, 282.
16 Ibid., 282, 319.
17 Ibid., 157, 284.
18 Ibid., 273–274, 286–287.
19 Ibid., 204–206.
20 Ibid., 290.

(also banned) foreign radio broadcasts for alternative perspectives. Using the branch's typewriter, Helmuth began producing handbills excoriating Hitler and his Nazi functionaries, and rebuking the submissive Germans who tolerated the slide into tyranny. He authored a total of twenty-nine pamphlets, frequently calling out peers he felt were failing. For example:

> German boys! Do you know the country without freedom, the country of terror and tyranny? Yes, you know it well, but are afraid to talk about it. They have intimidated you to such an extent that you don't dare talk for fear of reprisals. Yes you are right; it is Germany—Hitler Germany! Through their unscrupulous terror tactics against young and old, men and women, they have succeeded in making you spineless puppets to do their bidding.[21]

This confrontational approach would have surely been institutional suicide for the Church—just as it was for the Jehovah's Witness sect, which directly notified the Nazis that "there is a direct conflict between your law and God's law" and refused to render the Hitler salute to any person or flag.[22] For this refusal to comply, the Nazis criminalized their worship services, fired members from civil service jobs, and sent roughly half their members to prison and concentration camps, with thousands dying; more than 200 were formally executed.[23] Helmuth's obstinance was similarly grounded in

21 Alan Frank Keele and Blair Holmes, *When Truth was Treason: German Youth Against Hitler* (University of Illinois Press, 1995), 203.

22 *Moroni and the Swastika*, 95.

23 Ibid., 96.

religious conviction, but not supported by his own Church, which chose a quite opposing path in an effort to shield members and missionaries from attack. His branch president attempted to excommunicate him and shortly thereafter, now age seventeen, the Nazis executed him—giving him the unfortunate distinction of being the youngest person formally put to death by the Nazis.[24]

Few will dispute the prudence of the Church's strategy and the importance of picking one's battles. It does little good to one's self, family, congregation, or others to put up a quick fight and be summarily executed. It is perhaps for this reason that God stated that "this is wisdom, make unto yourselves friends with the mammon of unrighteousness, and they will not destroy you."[25] It follows the old adage of keeping your friends close and your enemies closer; there is strategic benefit in not incurring the wrath of a powerful foe.

But while strategy should be considered, one cannot claim that God forbids anything but servility to the state. Helmuth, for example, is widely praised as a freedom fighter—a brave and principled young man who stood up for his convictions and who sought to popularize the truth. Books, plays, movies, and other media extol his heroism.[26] It's easy to recognize

---

24 Ibid., 311–312.

25 D&C 82:22.

26 Not all of them were well received at the time. A popular theatrical production of Helmuth's story performed at BYU was shut down by Thomas S. Monson, who had been tasked with overseeing the Church's efforts regarding East Germany. When asked by an Associated Press reporter about his decision to shut it down, Monson replied: "Who knows what was right or wrong then? I don't know what we accomplish by dredging these things up and trying to sort them out." See *Moroni and*

the virtue of his activism. And despite conflict with his own Church, Helmuth was doing what he thought God had commanded. "My Father in Heaven knows that I have done nothing wrong," he wrote in a letter just hours before his death. "I know that God lives, and He will be the proper judge of this matter."[27] Indeed, the scriptures support the very path this valiant Saint followed: "men should be anxiously engaged in a good cause, and do many things of their own free will, and bring to pass much righteousness";[28] "we should waste and wear out our lives in bringing to light all the hidden things of darkness, wherein we know them; and they are truly manifest from heaven";[29] and "it becometh every man who hath been warned to warn his neighbor."[30]

It may very well be that in its institutional form, God does want the Church to play nice and protect the flock. Church leaders may therefore be acting appropriately by pursuing a particular course that is more cautious around—and even friendly toward—evil people in positions of power. But their course of action need not necessarily be our own; members of the very same Church are not under implicit obligation to do as their leaders do. Indeed, one can argue that the Church "waits" for us to individually do what it cannot or should not.

---

the Swastika, 327.

27 Document 61, in Blair Holmes and Alan Keele, *When Truth Was Treason: German Youth against Hitler: The Story of the Helmuth Hübener Group* (Urbana: University of Illinois Press, 1995), 240. The original letter was lost. Helmuth's words are Marie Sommerfeld's re-creation from memory.

28 D&C 58:27.

29 D&C 123:13.

30 D&C 88:81.

One General Authority Seventy, Craig C. Christensen, stated as much at a conference for Church apologists and scholars. "You're not the Church," he told them. "And you can say things that we can't say." He continued:

> One of the blessings and one of the missions that you are able to take are issues that the Church doesn't take. And so we work in tandem. If you look like an extension of the Church, you wouldn't have the power to do what you need to do.
>
> As we respond on the battle on the Internet, only about ten or fifteen percent can come from the Church. The rest has to come from partners... and other individual members to be engaged in the conversation.[31]

Whether right or wrong, it's clear that the Church indeed waits—it wants, or perhaps needs, individuals to step up and do what it cannot. Sadly, in our Church culture most members take their behavioral cues from the institution, and therefore mimic its inaction. But just as "it is not meet that [God] should command in all things,"[32] it follows that we should not expect the Church to direct our actions in all things either; its actions need not dictate our own. What Ezra Taft Benson said about the Constitution applies as well to broader problems in the night of wrong that men of God are called to rise up against:

---

31 @make.kenzie, "FAIR: The Second Pulpit of the Mormon Church," Video, July 23, 2023, https://www.tiktok.com/@make.kenzie/video/7259072038139104554.

32 D&C 58:26.

> And now as to the last neutralizer that the devil uses most effectively—it is simply this: "Don't do anything in the fight for freedom until the Church sets up its own specific program to save the Constitution." This brings us right back to the scripture opened with today—to those slothful servants who will not do anything until they are "compelled in all things." Maybe the Lord will never set up a specific church program for the purpose of saving the Constitution. Perhaps if he set one up at this time it might split the Church asunder, and perhaps he does not want that to happen yet, for not all the wheat and tares are fully ripe.[33]

We individuals must be the change we wish to see in the world. We are catalysts for action, not passive robots programmed to compliantly execute the wishes of our institutional masters. Institutional prudence is not a ceiling on personal duty. When truth needs telling, victims need defending, or darkness needs exposing, don't wait for a program, a memo, or a press release—study, pray, and act. Let the institutional Church do what it must; let free men and disciples of Christ do what they ought. The Church waits while God's kingdom moves at the speed of our initiative.

Make the Church Great

Merrill's lyrics suggest not only that the Church waits for us, but that it does so because its strength is unequal to its task. In view of this imbalance, he called upon men of God to

33 Ezra Taft Benson, *An Enemy Hath Done This* (Salt Lake City: Parliament Publishers, 1969) 278.

"rise up, and make her great!" But this call to action was met with derision by some denominational leaders who "objected to the hymn, because they have said that only God can make the church great," Merrill wrote. "To that I have answered that if anyone can show me a single instance in history where God has made the church great without using *men of God* to do it, I should be interested. No answer has ever come."[34]

And so Merrill may be right—the duty to make the Church great falls upon each individual's shoulders, particularly the men who compose God's priesthood. But what does this mean, exactly? How do we make an institution great? Are we to funnel even more tithes into the Lord's storehouse? Should we allocate more time to missionary work to fill the pews each Sunday with more members? Maybe we ought to share links to Church resources online to boost its social media profiles?

Perhaps we have an incorrect assumption leading to the wrong questions. Thus far we've considered the Church in an institutional context; it is an organization—more specifically, a registered corporate entity with property, staff, revenue streams, liabilities, and so on. But God, it seems, takes a far more expansive view. "Behold, this is my doctrine," He said to Joseph Smith in 1829, "whosoever repenteth and cometh unto me, the same is my church."[35] The Greek word *ekklesia*, and the Hebrew *qahal*, are both translated into modern language as "church" but are synonymous with "assembly"—a

34 Letter to Lester Hostelter, in *Handbook to the Mennonite Hymnary* (General Conference of the Mennonite Church of North America, 1949).

35 D&C 10:67.

group of people. It is not a building, a 501(c)(3), or a formal organization. It is the people alongside whom we covenant and commune. It's a network of individuals, each striving to love and follow God.

If the Church is more a community of Saints than an organized system of worship, how might that change Merrill's meaning? Suddenly making the Church great becomes less about behavior tied to an institution and more about fulfilling Christ's commandment to love one another and treat our neighbor as we would Him. If the Church is people, then greatness is not better program execution—it's better discipleship. Greatness looks like sharing truth boldly, offering charity directly, reconciling offenses quickly, consecrating time and treasure daily, praying meaningfully, serving others spontaneously, and teaching doctrine plainly. The Savior called us the "light of the world";[36] institutions don't shine—disciples do. Of course, by engaging in these Christlike behaviors the institution will benefit, but more importantly, the body of Christ will gain weight and reach. Merrill's charge lands here: rise up, not to polish an organization, but to enlarge a people—so faithful, so useful, so present in the lives of neighbors that God's Church is unmistakably "great" where it counts most.

Consider this question: Can greatness be the fruit of corruption? Of course not. Jesus was emphatic about the need for internal purity to match one's external actions. "Woe unto you, scribes and Pharisees, hypocrites!" He said. "For ye are like unto whited sepulchres, which indeed appear beautiful

---

36 Matthew 5:14.

outward, but are within full of dead men's bones, and of all uncleanness. Even so ye also outwardly appear righteous unto men, but within ye are full of hypocrisy and iniquity."[37] His prescription? "Cleanse first that which is within."[38] We see this approach in Captain Moroni. From the front lines he issued a blistering rebuke to the rulers in Zarahemla for neglect and corruption—and then put them on notice: repent and send aid, or he would leave the border war, march to the capital, and remove them himself.

> Now I would that ye should remember that God has said that the inward vessel shall be cleansed first, and then shall the outer vessel be cleansed also. And now, except ye do repent of that which ye have done, and begin to be up and doing, and send forth food and men unto us, and also unto Helaman, that he may support those parts of our country which he has regained, and that we may also recover the remainder of our possessions in these parts, behold it will be expedient that we contend no more with the Lamanites until we have first cleansed our inward vessel, yea, even the great head of our government.[39]

Our call to make the Church great—to produce actions worthy of being called a Saint—requires us to first cleanse our own inward vessel. We must not, like the scribes and Pharisees, act with any hypocrisy or iniquity; before we fight the night of wrong, we must root it out at home. Making the

37 Matthew 23:27–28.
38 Matthew 23:26.
39 Alma 60:23–24.

Church great, therefore, requires that *we* become great—clean, honest, disciplined, and repentant men whose private lives match their public witness. "Be ye clean that bear the vessels of the Lord"[40] is a commandment for a reason. This internal improvement is critical because only then do our warnings carry weight and our service carry power. A church cannot outpreach the secret sin of its men; corrupt individuals lead to a corrupted institution. Freedom from the bondage of sin is the launch pad for credible discipleship; our holiness unlocks the boldness, clarity, and charity required to change one's ward and the entire world. The Church waits; Zion rises only at the speed of our obedience to God.

---

40 D&C 38:42.

WHERE JESUS TROD

Say the word flower twenty times in a row. (Seriously, try it.) Toward the end, you may experience a common phenomenon where the word begins to lose its meaning. It may even start to sound strange or feel like a collection of sounds rather than a meaningful term. This well-studied effect is called semantic satiation and occurs when frequent repetition weakens our brain's response to the meaning associated with the term.

I wonder if the cultural normalization of key terms in the Church produces the same effect. "Choose the Right" was the popular refrain in the 1980s and 90s, with people (myself included) wearing the acronym on rings as purported daily reminders. In the 1960s, it was "Every member a missionary," and a decade later "Lengthen your stride" came onto the scene with force. More recently we've been bombarded with references to "covenant path" and "prophetic counsel."[1] The same holds true for the name of the Church's new curriculum, "Come, Follow Me."

---

1 I explore the frequency of these and more terms in Connor Boyack, "Changing Mormon Catchphrases," YouTube video, December 29, 2024, https://www.youtube.com/watch?v=JQPObr09oEc.

The title is taken from the story where a wealthy, powerful person inquired of Jesus what he must do to inherit eternal life. Here's the exchange:

> Thou knowest the commandments, Do not commit adultery, Do not kill, Do not steal, Do not bear false witness, Honour thy father and thy mother.
>
> And he said, All these have I kept from my youth up.
>
> Now when Jesus heard these things, he said unto him, Yet lackest thou one thing: sell all that thou hast, and distribute unto the poor, and thou shalt have treasure in heaven: and come, follow me.[2]

The Lord's invitation to follow Him permeates the scriptural record. To the fishermen Simon and Andrew, Jesus said, "Follow me, and I will make you fishers of men."[3] Passing by Matthew's tax booth, Jesus stopped and said "Follow me."[4] When He found Philip, the Lord said the same.[5] And to the gathered apostles, Jesus twice invited His chosen followers to follow Him.[6] No doubt this invitation was extended to other listeners following the Messiah during his mortal ministry; it remains extended to us. And despite the risk of semantic satiation by adopting these words as the official title of our Church curriculum, they contain significant meaning for those with ears to hear.

---

2 Luke 18:20–22; Matthew 19:16–21; Mark 10:17–21.
3 Matthew 4:19.
4 Matthew 9:9.
5 John 1:43.
6 John 21:19–22.

If we are to lift high the cross of Christ and tread where His feet have trod, as Merrill wrote, then we are signing up for a truly countercultural lifestyle that will put us at odds with nearly everyone around us. Jesus's teachings remain as divisive today as they were when taught among the Pharisees and scribes; His message sows division by creating contrast between those who follow and those who reject Him. Though one Church leader claimed that Christ "is the great unifier,"[7] Christ himself stated:

> Suppose ye that I am come to give peace on earth? I tell you, Nay; but rather division: For from henceforth there shall be five in one house divided, three against two, and two against three. The father shall be divided against the son, and the son against the father; the mother against the daughter, and the daughter against the mother; the mother in law against her daughter in law, and the daughter in law against her mother in law.[8]

He also said, "Think not that I am come to send peace on earth: I came not to send peace, but a sword."[9] Yes, unity is the ideal, but truth is paramount—and truth divides. As Nephi pointed out, "the guilty taketh the truth to be hard, for it

---

7 David L. Buckner, "Ye Are My Friends," October 2024 General Conference, https://www.churchofjesuschrist.org/study/general-conference/2024/10/25buckner. It is also interesting to note that over the past century there are scores of references from Church leaders to scriptures dealing with unity but only a single reference—from Dallin H. Oaks in 2009—to the verses where Christ highlights the implicit division that is associated with His message.

8 Luke 12:51–53.

9 Matthew 10:34.

cutteth them to the very center."[10] Following Christ, therefore, means standing up to those who traffic in deception and who prefer vain, flattering words to delude others into supporting them. This is why prophets have always been attacked by those they were sent to rebuke—Abinadi burned at the stake by King Noah,[11] Jeremiah imprisoned by the politicians his words threatened,[12] Enoch prophesying to the people who "hated" him,[13] Elijah being threatened with death by Jezebel,[14] Zechariah being stoned to death in the temple court[15]—and many more examples including, of course, Jesus of Nazareth. Treading where He trod means that we must promote truth in a world filled with lies—and that our reward will likely include persecution as well.

There are ample opportunities to send a spiritual sword by standing for truth: affirming the eternal identity of one's gender; refusing to support Caesar in order to only serve one Master; equating abortion with murder; opposing same-sex marriage; combating socialism and all coercive political ideologies; suggesting that many self-proclaimed Saints are as idolatrous as were the Pharisees; decrying feminism and highlighting its Marxist roots; and on and on. In short, those who would follow Christ must renounce the world and its prince—and those who follow that prince, whether consciously or not. Jesus told His disciples that each person must "deny himself

10 1 Nephi 16:2.
11 Mosiah 17:7–20.
12 Jeremiah 38:6.
13 Moses 6:31, 37.
14 1 Kings 19:1–2.
15 2 Chronicles 24:20–21.

and take up his cross and follow me."[16] But what does it mean to take up His cross? It is to "deny [ourselves] all ungodliness, and every worldly lust."[17] He then tells us to "forsake the world, and save your souls."[18] We cannot embrace Christ's counterfeits and the satanic influences behind them without corrupting ourselves. Following Jesus means leaving the world behind and avoiding all the related traditions and institutions that compete against Christ for our loyalty.

Consider a few concrete patterns from scripture. Daniel kept praying when a decree said otherwise—and went to the lions' den rather than mute his devotion.[19] Shadrach, Meshach, and Abednego refused to bow to Nebuchadnezzar's image—no hedging, no performative kneel—choosing a furnace over a false god.[20] Peter and the other apostles, hauled before the Sanhedrin, answered, "We ought to obey God rather than men."[21] None of them sought martyrdom; they simply would not betray the truth to purchase pretended peace.

Our test, however, is rarely so direct. Most days, no official demands that we bow or die. Instead, the pressure seeps in by degrees: a euphemism at work you're expected to repeat; a policy you quietly enable; a tax you vote for; entertainment you excuse; a social feed that escorts you away from the strait and narrow. The threats are slow, subtle, and wrapped in plausible reasons to comply. That is why following Christ now

---

16 Joseph Smith Translation, Matthew 16:25.
17 Joseph Smith Translation, Matthew 16:26.
18 Joseph Smith Translation, Matthew 16:29.
19 Daniel 6.
20 Daniel 3.
21 Acts 5:29.

requires a different vigilance: discerning the drift, naming it early, and reversing course before small compromises harden into a way of life.

The Slow Stain

Each year, an estimated 15,000 new self-help books are published, encouraging readers to set and accomplish goals to improve their life.[22] Hundreds of millions of copies of such books are in circulation, from *Think and Grow Rich* and *The Alchemist* to *Be Your Future Self Now* and *Atomic Habits*. We are, by our nature, goal-setting creatures; our action is directed toward things we desire. And as Christians, our self-stated ultimate goal is salvation and to return to God's presence—to receive a heavenly reward for passing our mortal probation.

That goal, however, is distant and abstract, while the rivals to it are near and concrete. As one writer suggested, "We are kept from our goals not by obstacles, but by a clear path to a lesser goal."[23] Spiritual drift rarely comes from open rebellion; it comes more often from choosing the clear path to a lesser goal—comfort, convenience, status, and more—again and again until priorities quietly invert. We don't bow to Babylon; we budget for it. We pledge loyalty to Christ on Sunday, then let conflicting priorities colonize the week. Inch by inch, the daily trade-offs teach our hearts what to love. This is the threat: not a single dramatic surrender, but a thousand small

---

22 "Self-Help Books Statistics," WordsRated, December 16, 2022, https://wordsrated.com/self-help-books-statistics/.

23 Robert Brault, *Round Up The Usual Subjects: Thoughts On Just About Everything* (CreateSpace, 2014), 185.

reallocations of attention and affection away from God toward idols that pay out quickly and demand worship gradually.

That attention, for many Latter-day Saints, was momentarily focused on this trend in 1995 when President Gordon B. Hinckley highlighted the prevailing "allurement and enticement to take on the slow stain of the world."[24] The scriptures are filled with examples of God's people embracing—slowly, then suddenly—the idolatrous ideas and corrupt behaviors of those who lived near and among them. Things were so bad in Noah's day that "God looked upon the earth, and, behold, it was corrupt; for all flesh had corrupted his way upon the earth."[25] The rescued Israelites embraced Egyptian paganism to the point of creating and worshiping a golden calf.[26] After settling in Canaan, they "followed other gods, of the gods of the people that were round about them and bowed themselves unto them."[27] Rejecting the prophetic judgment of Samuel, a later generation of Israelites demanded a monarchy "to judge us like all the nations."[28] King Solomon, influenced by his foreign wives, built high places for false gods, gradually integrating their religious rites into Israel's worship.[29] The northern kingdom of Israel incorporated idol worship and pagan rituals introduced by neighboring peoples.[30] The people of

---

24 Gordon B. Hinckley, "Stand Strong against the Wiles of the World," *Ensign*, November 1995, https://www.churchofjesuschrist.org/study/general-conference/1995/10/stand-strong-against-the-wiles-of-the-world.

25 Genesis 6:12.

26 Exodus 32:1–6.

27 Judges 2:12.

28 1 Samuel 8:5.

29 1 Kings 11:1–10.

30 2 Kings 17:7–17.

Judah adopted foreign idols and forsook their covenant. God had planted them "a noble vine, wholly a right seed," yet by adopting the beliefs of surrounding pagan cultures, they had "turned into the degenerate plant of a strange vine."[31] Jesus rebuked the Pharisees and scribes for clinging to the traditions of men and rejecting the commandments of God.[32] Paul warned of those who had "changed the glory of the uncorruptible God into an image made like to corruptible man."[33] The list goes on.

Of course, the slow spread of society's degenerate practices is not reserved for scripture stories of yesteryear; we, too, can be, and are, guilty of the same. President Hinckley's observation was not in the abstract. It's already happening, and we were warned of that outcome in revealed scripture. Nephi foresaw that in the latter days, many would be pacified into carnal security, their souls being led away "carefully down to hell."[34] Others would fall to flattery, being deceived into ignoring the devil's influence in their own lives, "until he grasps them with his awful chains."[35] Secret combinations seduced the once-righteous Nephites "until they had come down to believe in their works and partake of their spoils, and to join with them in their secret murders and combinations."[36] We are directly commanded by the Lord to "repent of [our] sins, and suffer not that these murderous combinations shall

31 Jeremiah 2:11–13, 20–23.
32 Mark 7:8–9.
33 Romans 1:23.
34 2 Nephi 28:21.
35 2 Nephi 28:22.
36 Helaman 6:38.

get above [us]." Moroni's warning makes clear this outcome is not a matter of if, but "*when* ye shall see these things come among you."[37] And in a revelation given to Joseph Smith, God lamented the many covenant breakers who "seek not the Lord to establish his righteousness, but every man walketh in his own way, and after the image of his own god, whose image is in the likeness of the world, and whose substance is that of an idol..."[38]

The antidote to these alluring side quests—the way we avoid the clear paths to lesser goals in life—is to walk where Jesus trod. He did not ask for occasional grand gestures; He asked for a cross taken up daily, for a narrow way walked one choice at a time. Following Him means reordering the ordinary—how we spend mornings and money, what we watch and welcome, who we listen to and laud. The drift is incremental; so, too, is the cure. But few choose to use it; it is more difficult than it appears to walk in Christ's footsteps. God Himself bemoaned this fact in the introductory revelation given to Joseph Smith in 1831:

> And the arm of the Lord shall be revealed; and the day cometh that they who will not hear the voice of the Lord, neither the voice of his servants, neither give heed to the words of the prophets and apostles, shall be cut off from among the people; For they have strayed from mine ordinances, and have broken mine everlasting covenant; They seek not the Lord to establish his

37 Ether 8:23–26.
38 D&C 1:15–16.

> righteousness, but every man walketh in his own way, and after the image of his own god, whose image is in the likeness of the world, and whose substance is that of an idol, which waxeth old and shall perish in Babylon, even Babylon the great, which shall fall.[39]

The whole of humanity is saturated in worldly ideas and practices, with most people choosing "not [to] endure sound doctrine; but after their own lusts shall they heap to themselves teachers, having itching ears; And they shall turn away their ears from the truth."[40] And because the stain is slow, most are easily able to convince themselves into believing that the syncretic religion they participate in—corrupted just enough to be compromised while retaining the outward appearance and performances of the original—is unadulterated in any way. This is why God began "a marvelous work"[41] to reintroduce His doctrine and reveal the correct path to pursue—the doctrinal steps one must actually walk to follow Jesus. This clarity was meant to dispel the confusion created by worldly creeds and councils that had encumbered the gospel. One would hope, then, that *this* time things would fare better; perhaps the "last days" dispensation could avoid the same, slow stain that had tainted God's past peoples. Yet the more things change, the more they seem to stay the same. Today's Church is no less susceptible to embracing the slow stain of the world than the ancient one.

---

39 D&C 1:14–16.
40 2 Timothy 4:3–4.
41 D&C 4:1.

What Would Jesus Do?

How, then, can we avoid the same fate? How can men of God—how can all of us—follow in Christ's footsteps and avoid the countless, wandering pathways that distract us from sticking to the strait and narrow? This is not an uncommon question. For example, at various times, it's been widely fashionable for young people to wear apparel and accessories featuring WWJD, standing for What Would Jesus Do? Church members in past years frequently wore CTR jewelry, reminding them to Choose the Right. And while these efforts also risk semantic satiation—becoming so familiar that they lose meaning and potency—they remind us of the need for daily reorientation toward God.

Perhaps one of the most crucial observations is that whatever the answers are, they are intended to permeate our entire lives; God's truths are not meant to be relegated to occasional mention during Church meetings and a few minutes of rushed family scripture study (if that even occurs). No, the profundities of the gospel of Jesus Christ are supposed to affect our daily lives—our interpersonal interactions, our economic choices, our political views, how we spend our time, what our thoughts focus on, and more. Christ's teachings are not talking points for Sabbath worship; they are a blueprint for building God's kingdom and our roles within it.

The early Christians recognized this. The followers Jesus attracted during His mortal ministry were not called Christians until years later in Antioch, as missionary work spread.[42] Previously, it appears that the manner of life practiced by disciples of Christ was simply called "the Way." As Jesus taught His flock about His impending return to heaven, Doubting Thomas said, "Lord, we know not whither thou goest; and how can we know the way?" Jesus replied, "I am the way."[43] This was taken at face value; the apostles came to understand that Christ's teachings were a set of instructions for returning to God's presence. Living how God taught was literally "the way" back to heaven. It is no surprise, then, that this is what the life Christ requires of us came to be called. Paul mentions that he previously persecuted "this Way"—those practicing this lifestyle—unto death.[44] Later, once converted to it, he sought after those who "belonged to the Way"[45] so that he might gather them to Jerusalem. As missionary work spread, "there arose a great disturbance about the Way."[46] Paul noted that the Jewish establishment considered "the Way" as "heresy,"[47] and Luke pointed out that the Roman governor at the time had a "knowledge of [the] Way."[48] Christianity is not a set of doctrines to be read about in books of scripture and superficially pondered in sporadic religious services. It is the way we ought to live.

42 Acts 11:26.
43 John 14:5–6.
44 Acts 22:4; New International Version.
45 Acts 9:2; New International Version.
46 Acts 19:23; New International Version.
47 Acts 24:14; New International Version.
48 Acts 24:22; New International Version.

What way should we follow? The answer is simple. "That which ye have seen me do," Jesus said, "even that shall ye do."[49] Like sheep, we are to follow the Shepherd's Way.[50] More than mere actions to replicate, though, Christ's words leave would-be disciples with instructions, which we must follow if we are to call ourselves disciples. If someone attacks us or threatens war, the world wants to escalate and seek vengeance; Christ calls on us to renounce war and proclaim peace.[51] In a world awash with pornography and prostituting "content creators," the world wants us to classify it as female empowerment, sexual liberation, and normalized expression; Christ condemns even so much as looking at a woman lustfully.[52] When Satan's mortal minions seek control of the levers of power to exempt themselves and their friends from legal consequence for theft and murder, the world wants us to brand as fringe conspiracy theorists those who even point out the problem; Christ commands us to "awake to a sense of your awful situation, because of this secret combination"[53] and to "waste and wear out our lives in bringing to light all the hidden things of darkness."[54] If someone is poor, the world wants us to push them to a taxpayer-funded program; Christ wants us to personally and voluntarily feed, clothe, and visit them.[55] And to achieve supposed success, the world wants us

49 3 Nephi 27:21.
50 John 10:27.
51 D&C 98:16, 23–32.
52 Matthew 5:27–28.
53 Ether 8:24.
54 D&C 123:13.
55 Matthew 25:35–40.

to worship mammon and build Babylon; Christ requires us to lay up our treasure in heaven and use the world's resources to build His kingdom.[56]

This is all much easier said than done. Jesus condemned as hypocrites those who "draweth nigh unto me with their mouth, and honoureth me with their lips; but their heart is far from me."[57] Isaiah, whom Jesus was quoting, adds this: "their fear toward me is taught by the precept of men."[58] We live in a world where talk is cheap and abundant; many profess Christ, though few walk where He trod. The precepts of men—the traditions of our fathers—have often reduced worship to simplistic statements that lack substance. We prefer milk to meat and embrace a faith that is weak and permissive of our varied political, economic, and personal beliefs and actions. Even those who wear the WWJD question on their body don't actually do what Jesus would do; wearing a CTR ring does not necessarily cause one to choose the right. "Narrow is the way which leadeth unto life, and few there be that find it," Jesus taught.[59] Yet "wide is the gate, and broad is the way, that leadeth to destruction, and many there be which go in thereat."[60]

This numerical imbalance was foreseen by Nephi: "Yea, they have all gone out of the way; they have become corrupted... they have all gone astray save it be a few, who are the humble followers of Christ; nevertheless, they are led, that in many instances they do err because they are taught by the

56 Matthew 6:19–24; Luke 12:15.
57 Matthew 15:7–9.
58 Isaiah 29:13.
59 Matthew 15:14.
60 Matthew 15:13.

precepts of men."[61] If we wish to be among the few, there is no choice other than to rise up and have done with lesser things; to give heart and mind and soul and strength to serve our King; to bring in the day of brotherhood and end the night of wrong; to make the Church great as we tread where His feet have trod. These are daily actions—the literal Way of Christ. We are, in effect, to become lifestyle ambassadors of Jesus—"to stand as witnesses of God at all times and in all things, and in all places that ye may be in, even until death."[62]

Following Jesus is not a slogan to wear; it is a schedule to keep. It means ordering our hours, money, media, and loyalties so they match His—denying self, loving enemies, telling the truth, giving in secret, keeping covenants, and choosing persuasion over coercion as we deal with our fellow man. It means acting as God would: feeding the hungry, rescuing the confused, exposing lies, and choosing peace. This is "the Way"—daily, deliberate, often costly—and it is how disciples become the light in a dark age. Living this way leads the day of brotherhood to dawn because we unite around truthful ideas and righteous actions; the Church stops waiting because we stop waiting; the night of wrong recedes because men of God refuse its bargains and become anxiously engaged in good causes of their own free will. We must tread where Jesus trod or else we'll be swept wherever the crowd wanders.[63]

---

61 2 Nephi 28:11, 14.
62 Mosiah 18:9.
63 Ephesians 4:14; James 1:6.

CONCLUSION

The concerns and calls to action in these pages have not been theoretical. We have traced the night of wrong and the day of brotherhood, the need to cleanse the inward vessel, to act without waiting to be compelled, and to tread where Christ trod. These are not mere abstractions. They are intended to be assignments. The stakes are personal and public at once: families fray or flourish by the same choices that build or bankrupt a congregation. Our private holiness either powers or paralyzes the furtherance of the Lord's work. This must be, then, more than an academic exercise. It is ideally more like a field manual for men who intend to live as disciples—who will renounce lesser things, unite in God's work, and move the kingdom from *waiting* to *advancing*. So let me conclude where the work really begins—in a life, not a theory.

I am the oldest of four boys. Shortly before I became a deacon at age twelve, my father was called by the bishop to be our ward's scoutmaster. He agreed, but with one condition: he would serve in this position provided that he would not be released from his position until his last boy had obtained his Eagle Scout award. (Given how hard it was to find willing people to serve in such a demanding calling, the bishop was obviously elated and readily agreed.) I was a late-blooming teenage boy more interested in comics and computers than in camping, canoeing, or cooking over a butane stove in the middle of nowhere. But the system laid out before me—with its merit badges, meetings, ranks, and uniforms—unquestionably pushed me outside my comfort zone and helped me mature.

Along with the basics like tying knots and wilderness survival, I learned far more enduring lessons: what leadership looks like; the importance of preparedness; the value of community service; and why we should be physically strong, mentally awake, and morally straight. I had (and have) some objections to the program: its proximity to militarism (its creator Robert Baden-Powell, a lieutenant general in the British Army, wanted to teach boys about reconnaissance and military scouting); its promotion of statism ("A Scout is loyal to the King" and his subordinates, Baden-Powell wrote. "He must stick to them through thick and thin against anyone who is their enemy, or who even talks badly of them."[1]); and the dependency the Church long had on an outside organization—neglecting, in the process, fully half of its young members. But there's little doubt that it was helpful in my own development as a teenage boy. It was a framework to aid in my maturity—scaffolding to guide my development and help me navigate those years better than I would have otherwise.

In a 2015 blog post I called for the Church to abandon the Boy Scouts—four years before it happened. "I'd love to see a Church program for both boys and girls that features many of Scouting's praiseworthy components, but with a Christian in-

---

1 "Scout Law," Wikipedia, accessed September 14, 2025, https://en.wikipedia.org/wiki/Scout_Law.

dividualist twist," I wrote in that article.[2] Here were the components I suggested:

- Regular camping and other outdoor adventure activities, with a focus on God as Creator, appreciation for the beauty of nature, and exploration of the abundance and diversity in the world around us.
- Weekly exposure to life skills from a variety of areas, taught by those with expertise and experience in the field.
- Fellowshipping with and service to fellow youth and others in the community.
- Discussion groups on how to be faithful to God, encouraging youth to share their struggles and support one another.
- Teamwork and leadership training opportunities, with a focus on building skills to build the kingdom of God.

The Church *did* create a new youth program to fill in the void left by the separation from the Boy Scouts of America. It has been, in a word, awful. Whereas before, boys had structure and scaffolding, now they—and their female peers—are adrift in a poorly organized and even more poorly executed program, if it can even be called that. I am not alone in that

---

2 "The LDS Church Should Abandon the Boy Scouts—But for the Right Reasons," Connor's Conundrums, August 2, 2015, https://connorboyack.com/blog/the-lds-church-should-abandon-the-boy-scouts-but-for-the-right-reasons/.

sentiment; every time I speak out about this topic I am bombarded with concerned comments from Church members struggling with their teen children—their boys in particular. They wonder where the support went and feel mostly alone in having to help their boys find (and find value in) challenge, achievement, and purpose. Consider just a few of the hundreds of comments I received on a podcast episode I did regarding this new youth program:[3]

- "My wife and I have been in youth callings for years and it's just getting worse and worse... The scouting program was not always perfect and left some of the boys behind who weren't interested, but we switched an imperfect system for essentially no system."
- "The new youth group is totally basically doing nothing for the youth! As mom of three teenagers, I feel like the church youth program has failed my children! It has no structure. Most of the time my boys just go play games..."
- "The poorest executed BSA program was a million times more effective than what we have now."
- "I was very worried when they rolled out the new program. We've now had almost a full cohort go through it, and the kids are not alright. It's rudderless. Our

3 "New Youth Program: Success or Failure?" Sunday Musings, December 15, 2024, https://www.youtube.com/watch?v=o61L0CtFh7o.

ward tries to have campouts but it's nothing like the rigor it used to be."

- "I didn't love the scouts but now I regret losing that because the young men have been totally shafted. I have three teenage sons and it has just been frustrating to watch. And a little heartbreaking."
- "I've felt very disappointed in the current church youth program that feels so devoid of structure that leaders and youth alike are confused as to where to even start."
- "I am raising four boys. Men need structure and brotherhood, not to set goals in private and have no oversight. They also need men to be their mentors, not another thing that their mommies nag them about. The new program is not very effective."

Men need obstacles to surmount. They need a foe to vanquish. They need a path laid out before them and to understand the rules of engagement. They need to be challenged, their courage tested. Human societies since time immemorial have had various ways and means of transitioning boys to men, often involving some spectacular challenge to commemorate that milestone. But today's boys—in and out of the Church—are adrift. They lack mentorship and designed struggle to strengthen them. They are taught some benign principles and told to lead themselves. They are largely rudderless. I say this not entirely as an outside observer; I'm the father of a teenage son, who for a period of time was also an adult leader in his quorum. The training was nearly nonexistent, the standards and expectations unclear; we were left to fill in large gaps with our own effort, yet I felt like I was pushing a boulder uphill. There was little to no effort from the other adult leaders, and with youth told to lead themselves, the activities they planned nearly always centered around entertainment. I regularly suggested things that would be challenging physically or intellectually, but there was nearly no interest. It was a maddening exercise to watch my efforts disregarded and to see my son being exposed to such spiritual, intellectual, physical, and social mediocrity.

This is a travesty because God's kingdom needs strong men—and little to no scaffolding for boys leads to weak and ineffectual men. God needs His sons to lean into their masculinity and use their strength in His service. And while the counsel throughout this book typically applies to all of God's children, male and female, we must take special concern in today's society for boys and men. "The current plight of boys and young men is, in fact, a women's issue," noted Christina Sommers, author of *The War Against Boys*. "Those boys are our sons; they are the people with whom our daughters will build a future. If our boys are in trouble, so are we all. In the war against boys, as in all wars, the first casualty is truth."[4]

The truth is that masculinity—strength, initiative, risk-bearing, and restraint—is healthy and necessary. But post-modern feminism and gender ideology pathologize it as toxic,

---

4 Christina Hoff Sommers, *The War Against Boys: How Misguided Policies are Harming Our Young Men* (New York: Simon and Schuster Paperbacks, 2013), 3.

producing passive or predatory men instead of virtuous ones. The truth is that fathers are indispensable. But modern culture treats dads as optional or laughable, normalizing fatherlessness and worsening outcomes for kids. The truth is that men are called to provide, protect, and preside by persuasion. But our culture caricatures presiding as domination, shames provision as patriarchy, and delegates protection to the state. The truth is that sexual discipline builds families and civilizations. But hookup culture sells consequence-free pleasure and launders abortion as empowerment. The truth is that brotherhood makes men better. But isolation, doomscrolling, and pornography sever men from social bonds that can help them help others. The truth is that men need rites of passage and hard things. But comfort culture and safetyism keep boys soft, aimless, and untested. The truth is that mentorship from good men shapes boys into men of God. But adult male presence is stripped from schools, youth spaces, and even homes. The truth is that greatness begins with cleansing the inward vessel. But hypocrisy teaches men to polish optics while rotting inside.

We are in a war not just against boys and men, but against truth and righteousness. The adversary wants us wallowing in lesser things, distracted by deviations from the Way that allow the night of wrong to spread. With our heart, soul, mind, and strength compromised, the kingdom tarries longer, the church waiting, its brotherhood neutered and weak. But we can—we must—rise above this. Over a century later, Merrill's words ring as true as ever. *Rise up, O men of God!*

ABOUT THE AUTHOR

Connor Boyack is the author of several dozen books, founder of a think tank that has changed over 100 laws, frequent public speaker, and outlaw beekeeper.

Connor is best known as author of the acclaimed Tuttle Twins book series which has sold over six million copies. The Tuttle Twins books teach kids (and their parents!) the ideas of a free society. He is also executive producer of the Tuttle Twins animated cartoon series inspired by the books.

A self-made entrepreneur, Connor not only talks the talk, but walks the walk as the founder and president of the Libertas Network, a series of initiatives that change hearts, minds, and laws to create a freer future. His leadership has led Libertas to innovate over a dozen legal reforms that were the first of their kind, changing the lives of millions of people.

Connor lives near Salt Lake City, Utah, with his wife and two homeschooled children.

Find his religious books for sale at SocialHarmony.org and all his other books at LibertasPress.com.

www.ingramcontent.com/pod-product-compliance
Lightning Source LLC
LaVergne TN
LVHW010611100826
845148LV00014B/2914

* 9 7 9 8 8 8 6 8 8 0 4 9 6 *